The 100 *Best*
Annuals

A PRACTICAL ENCYCLOPEDIA

The 100 Best
Annuals

A PRACTICAL ENCYCLOPEDIA

PREVIOUSLY PUBLISHED AS PART OF *THE 400 BEST GARDEN PLANTS*

ELVIN McDONALD

RANDOM HOUSE   NEW YORK

A Packaged Goods Incorporated Book

Published in the United States by
Random House, Inc.
201 E. 50th Street
New York, NY 10022

Conceived and produced by
Packaged Goods Incorporated
276 Fifth Avenue, New York, NY 10001
A Quarto Company

Text and photography by Elvin McDonald
Designed by Yasuo Kubota, Kubota & Bender

Library of Congress Cataloging-in-Publication Data
The 100 best annuals: a practical encyclopedia
Elvin McDonald.

p. cm.

Includes index.
ISBN 0-679-76027-X
1. Plants, Ornamental—Encyclopedias. 2. Plants,
Ornamental—Pictorial works. 3. Gardening—
Encyclopedias. 4. Gardening—Pictorial works.
I. Title. II. Title: The one hundred best annuals.
III. Title: A practical encyclopedia.

SB407.M26 1995
35.9—dc20 94-35385

Random House website address: http://www.randomhouse.com/
Color separations by Hong Kong Scanner Arts Int'l Ltd.
Printed and bound in Singapore by Khai Wah-Ferco Pte. Ltd.
98765432
First Edition

Acknowledgments

Dedicated to Marta Hallett

Thanks to the home team, pals, and friends, particularly:

Kristen Schilo, editor; Mary Forsell, copyeditor;
Sarah Krall, assistant editor; Yasuo Kubota, designer;
Tatiana Ginsberg, production manager; Amy Detjen,
assistant production editor; Catherine San Filippo,
proofreader; Lillien Waller, helping hand; Carla Glasser, agent;
Douglas Askew, research; Tom Osborn, driver/gardener;
Rosalind Creasy, focalizer; James R. Bailey, neighbor;
Janis Blackschleger, telekineticist; Diane Ofner,
gardening student; JoAnn Trial, scientist, and Don Trial,
teacher; R. Michael Lee, architect; Charles Gulick,
gardener; Michael Berryhill, poet; Linda Starr, head
coach; Hila Paldi, body coach; Mark Inabnit, Publisher
and Editor-in-Chief, *Houston Life*; David Walker,
Editorial Director, *Houston Life*; Catherine Beason, angel
unaware; Maria Moss, Executive Editor, *Houston Life*;
David Warren, artist/gardenmaker; Audrey Scachnow,
tweak expressionist; Christy Barthelme, envisionary; Tino
and Richard, Stark Cleaning Services; Tony Williams, yard
man; Dan Twyman, pruner; and Leslie Williams, cheering.

Elvin McDonald
Houston, Texas
January 1, 1997

Contents

Introduction

The one hundred plants that appear in these colorful pages represent my pick of the crop as a lifelong gardener and horticultural journalist. They are far from being the only "best" plants. Some vast families and categories certainly deserve more attention. Most assuredly, I am already growing the plants and assembling the photography for a sequel. One of the most wonderful aspects of gardening is that we can never know all of the plants. For this reason, dedicated gardeners will always experience the thrill of the hunt, the excitement upon discovering a flower or plant more beguiling than could have been imagined.

How to Read an Entry

Within this book, plants appear in alphabetical order by botanical genus name. If you know only the plant's common name, look for it in the Index. The botanical name and its suggested pronunciation are followed by the common name or names, many of which are interchangeable, and then by the plant's family name, appearing first in botanical Latin and finally in English. For example, plants of the annual genus *Abelmoschus* (botanical name) are commonly referred to as flowering okra (common name). They are members of the Malvaceae (botanical family name), or mallow family (common family name).

Within the entries, species names sometimes appear, where applicable. For instance, in the *Salvia*, or sage, entry, the species names *S. splendens, S. farinacea,* and *S. coccinea* appear. All are broadly referred to as sage. Oftentimes, species do not have common names and, as a result, are known in the plant trade only by their botanical names.

In all, one hundred different plants are pictured in this volume, yet many more are actually named, a resource unto itself for tracking down worthwhile species and cultivars.

Within each entry, there is also a guide for cultivation:

Height/habit: Despite the inexactness of horticulture and botanical differences, I sum up here as much as can be said about a genus in as few words as possible.

Leaves: Many plants are appreciated for their foliage as much as—or even more so—than their flowers. Here I provide a succinct description of leaf shapes and characteristics.

Flowers: Dimensions, arrangement, and color and fragrance characteristics are noted.

Season: The plant's high season appears here.

When to plant: I have used the phrase "Set out transplants when available" for nearly all plants in the book. In other words, if a gardener shops regularly for plants, both through mail order and locally (at nurseries, garden centers, and plant auctions held by public gardens), they will be delivered or sold at approximately the correct planting time for that person's hardiness zone. Containerization, lightweight growing mediums, remarkably efficient distribution, and computerization have revolutionized the plant business. Yes, there are still plants shipped at the wrong time and local retailers who sell inappropriate choices, but on the whole, the system works.

I have also provided each plant's tolerance for cold and heat according to zone, as it appears on the United States Department of Agriculture's Plant Hardiness Zone Map (see page 112). (This information can also appear under "Season," if applicable.) However, please note that the U.S.D.A. map has traditionally been based on cold tolerance, not heat. Now the billion-dollar industry of gardening is working to generate maps and zone awareness for heat as well as cold, also taking into account the relative dryness or wetness of a particular climate. To establish heat tolerance zones for this book, I have used a variety of references, including the catalogs of Louisiana Nursery, Wayside Gardens, and Yucca Do Nursery (see Resources). I have also consulted the books listed in the Bibliography, especially *A Garden Book for Houston* and *Hortica*. When in doubt, ask a neighbor who

gardens for details about your hardiness zone. There are lots of variables and a host of gardeners who like nothing better than trying to succeed with a plant that is not rated for their zone.

Light: To prosper, most plants need strong light or some sun, in a site that affords air movement. Here, I provide specific light or shade requirements.

Soil: Most plants need well-drained soil that is kept evenly moist to on the dry side. There are rainy seasons when gardens are wet for long periods of time. If water stands for more than a few hours in your yard, this does not bode well for gardening—unless you are undertaking a water or bog garden. There are also dry seasons, and gardeners today generally subscribe to the concept of Xeriscaping: not to set in motion any garden that will require undue irrigation during normal times of drought.

Fertilizer: Generally speaking, 5-10-5 and 15-30-15 are good for flowering-fruiting plants. Timed-release 14-14-14 is an all-purpose, long-serving (up to a whole season from one application) fertilizer for a wide variety of plants. For acid-loving plants, choose 30-10-10 or chelated iron. Careful, consistent application of these or entirely organic fertilizers will result in vigorous growth.

Uses: Under this heading, each plant's strong points are discussed, though you the gardener may find your own unique usages.

As much as I can provide detailed information about the art of gardening, you will be your own best teacher, a philosophy stated most eloquently in this old garden verse:

> *If you seek answers,*
> *leave your questions*
> *outside the garden gate.*

Elvin McDonald
Houston, Texas   January 1, 1997

Chapter One
The Annual Garden

*A*nnuals can truly make the garden. They are the scented, flowering plants that enter the picture at the beginning of one growing season and exit by its end, having grown up from seeds into a new generation of blooms. Once they have returned to seed, they die back to the ground.

This wonderful rainbow of plants offers instant gratification, especially when purchased already blooming in packs of transplants. When a yard looks bleak, a patio pot bereft of hopeful signs, annuals are the ticket, a convenient way to color in the garden and focus on the bright side.

Annuals are the answer to an intrepid beginner's prayer. They encourage us to let go, to get on with the planting and not be paralyzed by questions about the unknown. They permit the gardener to try various planting and design ideas without the expense, hard work, or long-range commitment required by perennials and woody specimens.

Like many plants, annuals are extraordinarily adaptable. Usually they fail to do well only if the site poses extremes: whether too sunny or shady, too wet or dry, too hot or cold. Even if the plant does not fare well, it could still have a second life: though annuals complete their lives in one garden cycle, they have the potential to quickly regenerate from seeds, keeping your garden budget intact.

Planning and Designing the Annual Garden

You can make a garden entirely with annuals or feature them in special roles, whether as star players or mere extras in the company of all other classes of plants: bulbs and shrubs, trees and ground covers, perennials and vines, vegetables, fruits, and herbs.

Annuals and various tender or quick-to-bloom perennials treated as annuals run the gamut from edgers, creepers, and ground covers to hedgers, quick screeners, and viners and bloom variously from spring until fall. In zone 9 and warmer, an exciting array blooms through winter and

into spring, then goes to seed and dies rapidly at the onset of torrid summer weather. To plan your garden, look through Chapter Two to find the most appealing choices in color combinations and to decide which annuals best correspond to your own personal uses, whether in bouquets, to cover a trellis, or to act as ground covers.

"Mass for effect" is the number one rule for getting the most from annuals. Their impact is diminished by lining in a single row or by spotting here and there randomly or regularly, polka-dot style. Whether different colors and different shapes or textures are mixed or matched is largely a matter of personal taste. Whatever gives you pleasure is probably correct for your garden.

One of the easiest ways to feel success with a garden is to organize according to color. The all-white garden is one of the most romantic, but it also has a simplicity and gives a sense of order. By direct contrast, there are gardeners who wouldn't be happy without a fiesta mix of every flower color imaginable. The wise gardener Gertrude Jekyll noted that "...the blue garden needn't be all blue, merely beautiful."

Soil Preparation

Above all, annuals need well-drained soil. Don't plant them in ground where water stands several hours or overnight following rain. If you grow them in containers, be sure they have drain holes. So long as the soil is well drained, any site can be made hospitable.

To prepare the garden, dig ground beds the depth of a garden spade. Remove any weeds, clumps or runners of lawn grass, sticks, stones, and other debris. Top-dress with fertilizer, preferably an organic product. Add 2 to 6 inches (5 to 15 centimeters) of well-rotted compost. Fork, turn, rake, or till all of this together. Ideally this needs to stand a week or two to cure, but if you are in a hurry, soil preparation and planting can be done the same day.

If you are planting annuals in containers, the rule of thumb is the bigger the pot, the better the plant. Small pots outdoors don't fare well since they are prone to overheating and underwatering. Use fresh potting soil each season, or at least top-dress with well-rotted compost every year.

Buying and Planting Annuals

Gardeners at all stages from rank beginner to seasoned veteran will always grow certain plants from seeds. However, this takes extra planning. For quicker results, you might want to rely mostly on transplants started by professional growers and offered for sale at retail when blooms are in evidence.

One advantage of starting with plants coming into flower is that you can mix and match colors on the spot. Transplants are offered for as long a season as feasible in each region. This means you don't necessarily have to do all of your planting at once. Buying in installments can help you be a better, more satisfied gardener.

By the time transplants reach retail, the containers in which they are growing are already packed with roots. This can mean thorough watering daily or they may be permanently stunted. Therefore, it might be better not to bring plants home until you are actually ready and able to set them in permanent places.

After soil preparation, the next step to success with annual transplants is promptly to set each in place, teasing out the roots from the original soil mass so that they are able to make contact with the endemic soil. Set at the same level in the ground as they were growing previously in the container. Water well. In the event you are transplanting a seedling and the soil falls away, exposing the roots to air and light, set it quickly and gently into moist soil, then water well and provide shade from direct sun until the roots have time—a few days—to reestablish.

If you wish to start annuals from seed, keep in mind that seed packets are somewhat less reliable as indicators of proper planting time since they can be purchased year-round through catalogs and from local racks. Seeds for annuals that bloom in the spring are usually sown the previous fall or winter in mild regions and greenhouses. Seeds for summer through fall annuals can often be sown where they are to grow and bloom in the garden or containers as soon as the ground is warm and the weather settled in spring.

The easiest way to start annuals from seeds is to sow them on the site where they will grow and bloom. Prepare the soil, then sow in a natural drift or in short rows according to the space and your plan. In a mixed garden it is often possible to start seeds in a place protected a bit by the next-door perennial or shrub. This improvised nursery plot may be outlined with sand or a dribble of vermiculite, just to remind you or your helper to take special care.

The annuals that self-sow, or "volunteer," are among every gardener's favorites. They are often planted first in one place, but in succeeding seasons their charm is one of serendipity, popping up where we'd least expect to see them. Moreover, self-sown seedlings have a way of taking root and growing marvelously in nooks and crevices where setting a proper transplant would be impossible.

Caring for Annuals Throughout the Seasons

Be sure to give your annuals well-drained soil and the proper amounts of sun or shade, as indicated in Chapter Two. Additionally, provide adequate water from rain and irrigation, as well as fertilizer. With all of these elements in balance, the only routine cares for annuals are to remove the spent flowers before seeds form and to stake up any that have gotten too tall to stand on their own. Insects and diseases are hardly a consideration, with a few exceptions (see Chapter Three).

Essential Tools

Growing, showing, and in general enjoying annual flowers requires hardly any tools. Transplants in particular are perfect for town-house gardeners or anyone whose space is limited. It is nice to have a trowel and some hand pruners of the by-pass variety (with blades arranged more or less as scissors). Bamboo stakes or twiggy brush saved from general yard cleanup come in handy for holding or guiding growth, along with green twist-ties, jute garden twine, or raffia for securing branches to supports.

Year-round Gardening Calendar

Note planting reminders in a datebook or on a wall calendar. Become familiar with the United States Department of Agriculture Plant Hardiness Zone Map, which will help you learn the effects of cold on plants. Gardeners in zone 8 and colder to zone 3 in parts of the United States and Canada enjoy some annuals along with the spring bulbs, shrubs, and flowering trees. The greatest show usually takes place throughout summer, with a final flourish before frost by 'Sensation' cosmos and annual types of chrysanthemum.

Gardeners in zone 9 and warmer, from subtropical to tropical, depend on a different group of annuals for each season, with major plantings occurring in fall or early winter for blooms through spring, and again in late spring with plants that thrive in torrid conditions. The particular needs of each annual are noted with the individual descriptions in Chapter Two.

needs to be watered, see if it feels dry 3 to 4 inches (7.5 to 10 centimeters) down.

Bring spring annual bouquets indoors.

Deadhead spent blooms.

SUMMER:

Continue weeding, watering, and deadheading.

Sow seeds of late-blooming annuals.

Bring summer annual bouquets indoors.

Here is a calendar of seasonal reminders:

SPRING:

Till and prepare soil in garden beds and top-dress with fertilizer.

Sow seeds of annuals or transplant seedlings after danger of frost has passed.

Bring transplants to the garden.

Mulch with organic matter.

Start a gardening watering schedule, soaking soil thoroughly yet infrequently as a conservation measure. To check if soil

FALL:

Continue watering, weeding, and deadheading.

Bring late summer/early fall annual bouquets indoors.

In warm climates, sow annual seeds for spring blooms.

WINTER:

Begin designing your annual garden on paper.

Order everything you'll need: tools, seeds, flats, starting mixes.

Start annual seeds indoors.

Chapter Two
The 100 Best Annuals for Your Garden

ABELMOSCHUS
(able-MOS-kus)

Flowering Okra

MALVACEAE; mallow family

Height/habit: Spreading bushes, 1–6 ft. (30–180 cm.).
Leaves: Palmate, 3–12 in. (7.5–30 cm.) across.
Flowers: Round, 3–5 in. (7.5–12.5 cm.) across; pink, red, rose, or yellow; open fresh daily.

Season: Summer.
When to plant: Sow seeds indoors at 75–80°F (24–26°C) 12–16 weeks before frost-free weather. Set out transplants when available. Often reseeds zone 7 and warmer.
Light: Sun half day or more.
Soil: Well drained, moist.
Fertilizer: 5-10-5.
Uses: Beds, borders, pots.

ABUTILON
(ab-YEW-till-on)
Flowering Maple
MALVACEAE; mallow family

Height/habit: Upright varieties, 3–4 ft. (1–1.2 m.) on lightly woody stems; lax-stemmed varieties spread and cascade 2–3 ft. (61–90 cm.).

Leaves: Maple-shaped, 2–3 in. (5–7.5 cm.) across.

Flowers: Bell-shaped, hanging, 1–3 in. (2.5–7.5 cm.) across; most colors except blue.

Season: Summer in cold climates; all year zone 9 and warmer. Flowers on new growth when nights are at least 10°F (about 3–5°C) cooler than days.

When to plant: Sow seeds indoors at 70–75°F (21–24°C) 12–16 weeks before frost-free weather. Root tip cuttings winter through spring in a warm, sunny place. Set out transplants when available.

Light: Sun half day or more.

Soil: Well drained, moist.

Fertilizer: Alternate 30-10-10 with 15-30-15.

Uses: Beds, borders, pots, bouquets.

AGERATUM
(adj-er-RAY-tum)

Flossflower

COMPOSITAE; daisy family

Height/habit: Bedding varieties, 8-12 in. (20–30 cm.); cut-flower varieties 2 ft. (61 cm.).

Leaves: Lightly quilted, 2 in. (5 cm.) long.

Flowers: Fuzzy, flattened clusters, 2–4 in. (5–10 cm.) across; exceptional blues, also pink and white.

Season: Summer in cold climates; winter until spring zone 9 and warmer.

When to plant: Sow seeds indoors at 70–75°F (21–24°C) 8–12 weeks before planting-out weather; sow outdoors where they are to grow and bloom when soil is warm. Seeds need light to sprout; do not cover. Set out transplants when available.

Light: Sun half day or more.

Soil: Well drained, moist.

Fertilizer: 5-10-5.

Uses: Beds, borders, pots, bouquets.

AMARANTHUS
(am-uh-RANTH-us)

Joseph's Coat; Tampala; Love-lies-bleeding

AMARANTHACEAE; amaranth family

Height/habit: Upright, 2–8 ft. (61–240 cm.).

Leaves: Long or oval, 2–4 in. (5–10 cm.) long, beginning green or dark red, turning at the tops to bright yellow, orange, or phosphorescent pink.

Flowers: Tiny, dry, of little consequence in varieties having colorful leaves, such as Joseph's coat (*A. tricolor* 'Splendens') and tampala (*A. tricolor*); hanging panicles in curiously showy, wine red, or chartreuse on love-lies-bleeding (*A. caudatus*).

Season: Summer until fall frost; all zones.

When to plant: Sow seeds indoors at 70–75°F (21–24°C) 6–8 weeks before frost-free weather; outdoors as soon as soil is warm and there is no danger of frost. Set out transplants when available.

Light: Sun half day or more.

Soil: Well drained, moist.

Fertilizer: None required. Overly rich soil could result in less colorful leaves.

Uses: Beds, borders, pots, bouquets.

ANTIRRHINUM
(an-tir-EYE-num)
Snapdragon
SCROPHULARIACEAE; figwort family

Height/habit: Dwarf varieties in mounds, 8–12 in. (20–30 cm.); standard ('Maximum') types, 2–5 ft. (61–150 cm.).

Leaves: Lanceolate or oblong to 3 in. (7.5 cm.); pale green to reddish.

Flowers: Pouched to 2 in. (5 cm.) long in terminal racemes; most colors except blue. Deadheading increases bloom.

Season: Summer until hard frost in cold climates; winter until spring zone 9 and warmer.

When to plant: In the North, sow seeds indoors 70°F (21°C) 12–16 weeks before planting-out weather in the spring; in the South, sow seeds late summer through early fall. Prechill seeds in refrigerator 1 week before sowing. Seeds need light to sprout; do not cover. After sprouting, grow in cool temperature, about 45–50°F (7–10°C) to produce strong seedlings. Set out transplants when available.

Light: Sun half day or more.

Soil: Well drained, moist.

Fertilizer: 5-10-5.

Uses: Beds, borders, pots, bouquets.

ARCTOTIS
(ark-TOH-tiss)

African Daisy

COMPOSITAE; daisy family

Height/habit: Spreading, 6–18 in. (15–45 cm.) high/wide.
Leaves: Rosettes, pinnately lobed, to 6 in. (15 cm.) long.
Flowers: Single, to 2 in. (5 cm.) across; most colors except blue, from pastel to bright tones.
Season: Summer until frost in cold climates; fall until spring zone 9 and warmer.

When to plant: Sow seeds indoors at 60–70°F (15–21°C) 6–8 weeks before planting-out weather; sow outdoors where they are to grow and bloom when soil is warm.
Light: Sun half day or more.
Soil: Well drained, moist to dry; tolerates drought.
Fertilizer: 5-10-5.
Uses: Beds, borders, ground cover, rock gardens, pots.

BEGONIA
(be-GO-nee-ah)

Wax Begonia

BEGONIACEAE; begonia family

Height/habit: *B. semperflorens* in tidy, upright mounds, 6–18 in. (15–45 cm.).

Leaves: Oval, 1–3 in. (2.5–7.5 cm.) across; cupped, waxy; bright green, olive, or reddish bronze.

Flowers: Small clusters from the leaf axils, 1–2 in. (2.5–5 cm.) across; single if from seeds, double in certain cultivars propagated vegetatively; pink, red, rose, or white.

Season: Summer until frost in cold climates; year-round zone 9 and warmer.

When to plant: Sow seeds indoors at 70°F (21°C) 16 weeks before first blooms. Though tiny, seeds sprout readily when sown in moist medium. Seeds need light to sprout; do not cover. Set out transplants when available.

Light: Full sun to part shade.

Soil: Well drained, moist to slightly dry.

Fertilizer: 5-10-5.

Uses: Beds, borders, pots.

BELAMCANDA
(bell-am-KAN-dah)

Blackberry Lily; Leopard Flower

IRIDACEAE; iris family

Height/habit: Upright, 2–4 ft. (61–120 cm.).

Leaves: Resemble German iris; grow in flattened fans 1–1.5 ft. (30–45 cm.) long/wide.

Flowers: Single, 6 petals, to 2 in. (5 cm.) across; orange with red spots. Candy lily (*Pardancanda*) closely related, with same habit, but flowers in many pastel shades, often bicolored.

Season: Late summer until early fall, followed by seed clusters resembling large blackberries. Thrives in zone 5.

When to plant: Sow seeds indoors at 70°F (21°C) 8–12 weeks before planting-out weather; sow outdoors when soil is warm. Set transplants when available. Technically a rhizomatous bulb/perennial, but blooms reliably the first year from seeds.

Light: Sun half day or more.

Soil: Well drained, moist.

Fertilizer: 5-10-5.

Uses: Beds, borders, pots, seed heads for arrangements.

BORAGO
(boh-RAY-go)

Borage

BORAGINACEAE; borage family

Height/habit: Upright, sprawling, 1–2 ft. (30–61 cm.) high/wide.
Leaves: Hairy, pebbled, oblong, to 6 in. (15 cm.).
Flowers: Starry, 5-pointed, to 1 in. (2.5 cm.) across; blue.
Season: Summer until frost in cold climates; variously through the year zone 8 and warmer. Reseeds.
When to plant: Prechill seeds in refrigerator 1 week before planting. Sow seeds outdoors where they are to grow and bloom when soil is workable but cool.
Light: Sun half day or more.
Soil: Well drained; moist to on the dry side; tolerates drought.
Fertilizer: 5-10-5.
Uses: Beds, borders, herb gardens, bee plant, pots.

BRACHYCOME
(BRACKY-comb)

Swan River Daisy

COMPOSITAE; daisy family

Height/habit: Mounds, 6–10 in. (15–25 cm.).
Leaves: Finely dissected, fernlike, to 2 in. (5 cm.) long, growing mostly from the base.
Flowers: Nickel-sized daisies; various shades of blue, occasionally white; centers can be yellow or nearly black.
Season: Summer until frost in cold climates; winter until spring zone 9 and warmer.
When to plant: Sow seeds indoors at 70°F (21°C) 6–8 weeks before planting-out weather in spring; sow outdoors where they are to grow and bloom as soon as soil is warm and there is no danger of frost. Set out transplants when available.
Light: Sun half day or more.
Soil: Well drained, moist.
Fertilizer: 5-10-5.
Uses: Edging, rock gardens, pots.

BRASSICA
(BRASS-ick-ah)

Ornamental or Flowering Cabbage; Kale

CRUCIFERAE; mustard family

Height/habit: Symmetrical rosettes, 1–1.5 ft. (30–45 cm.) high/wide.

Leaves: Rounded (cabbage) or lacy (kale); blue-green at first, changing from the centers outward to white, cream, chartreuse, pink, or lavender.

Flowers: Yellow, 4-petaled, dime-sized, ascending gracefully above the leaves in spring until early summer.

Season: Best leaf coloration occurs in cool weather: fall in the North, fall until early spring zone 7 and warmer.

When to plant: Sow seeds 60–70°F (15–21°C) late spring until early summer in the North, late summer in mild climates. Seeds need light to sprout; a scant covering of horticultural vermiculite helps maintain desired moisture during germination. Set transplants when available.

Light: Sun half day or more.

Soil: Well drained, moist.

Fertilizer: 5-10-5. Too much nitrogen delays coloration.

Uses: Beds, borders, pots, arrangements.

BROWALLIA
(broh-WALL-ee-ah)

Bush Violet

SOLANACEAE; nightshade family

Height/habit: Mounds, 10–16 in. (25–40 cm.).

Leaves: Oval, 2–3 in. (5–7.5 cm.) long.

Flowers: 5-lobed stylized stars, 1–2 in. (2.5–5 cm.) across; blue or white.

Season: Spring until fall; through winter in sunny climes with temperatures of 55–70°F (13–21°C), zone 9–10.

When to plant: Sow seeds indoors at 70–72°F (21–22°C) 10–12 weeks before frost-free weather. Seeds need light to sprout; do not cover. After sprouting, grow at 55°F (13°C) and keep on dry side in early stages. Set out transplants when available.

Light: Mostly sun in cool weather, more shade in heat.

Soil: Well drained, moist.

Fertilizer: 5-10-5.

Uses: Beds, borders, pots, hanging baskets.

CALENDULA
(kal-END-yew-lah)

Pot Marigold

COMPOSITAE; daisy family

Height/habit: Dwarfs in mounds, 8–12 in. (20–30 cm.); cutting varieties, 14–30 in. (35–75 cm.).

Leaves: Oblong, 3–6 in. (7.5–15 cm.) long.

Flowers: 2–4 in. (5–10 cm.) across, atop straight stems; cream, orange, or yellow. Deadheading increases bloom.

Season: Late spring to frost in the North; fall until spring zone 9 and warmer. Cool nights, with temperatures of 45–55°F (7–13°C), favor quality.

When to plant: In the North, sow seeds indoors at 70°F (21°C) 6–8 weeks before planting-out weather in spring; provide continual darkness until seeds sprout; sow outdoors where they are to grow and bloom as soon as soil can be worked. In mild climates, sow seeds late summer until early fall. Set transplants when available.

Light: Sun half day or more.

Soil: Well drained, moist.

Fertilizer: 5-10-5.

Uses: Beds, borders, pots, bouquets.

CALLISTEPHUS
(kal-is-STEE-fuss)

China Aster; Annual Aster

COMPOSITAE; daisy family

Height/habit: Dwarf bedding varieties in mounds, 8–16 in. (20–40 cm.); cutting varieties, 16–30 in. (40–75 cm.).
Leaves: Broad or triangular ovals, 3–4 in. (7.5–10 cm.) long, mostly in basal rosettes.
Flowers: Single or double, 2–4 in. (5–10 cm.) across; blue, lavender, pink, red, rose, or white.
Season: Summer in cold climates; late spring until early summer zone 8 and warmer.

When to plant: Sow seeds indoors at 70°F (21°C) 6–8 weeks before planting-out weather in spring; sow outdoors where they are to grow and bloom as soon as soil is warm. Set transplants when available.
Light: Sun half day or more.
Soil: Well drained, moist. Avoid extremes of wet and dry. Do not grow China asters on the same site every year.
Fertilizer: 5-10-5.
Uses: Dwarfs for bedding and pots. Tall varieties for beds, borders, and bouquets.

CAPSICUM
(KAP-sick-um)

Ornamental Pepper

SOLANACEAE; nightshade family

Height/habit: Tidy, bushy, many branches, 10–18 in. (25–45 cm.) high/wide.
Leaves: Ovate or lanceolate, 1–2 in. (2.5–5 cm.) long.
Flowers: Starry, to .5 in. (1.2 cm.) across; white, followed by conical, fingerlike, or round peppers; green, chartreuse, cream, orange, red, or purple.

Season: Late summer until frost; fall until winter in frost-free zones (9-10).
When to plant: Sow seeds indoors at 70°F (21°C) 6–8 weeks before planting-out weather; sow outdoors where they are to grow and bloom when soil is warm. Set transplants when available.
Light: Sun half day or more.
Soil: Well drained, moist.
Fertilizer: 5-10-5.
Uses: Beds, borders, pots.

CATHARANTHUS
(kath-uh-RANTH-us)

Madagascar Periwinkle; Annual Vinca

APOCYNACEAE; dogbane family

Height/habit: Mounds, 6–18 in. (15–45 cm.).
Leaves: Oblong, lanceolate, 1–2 in. (2.5–5 cm.) long.
Flowers: 1–2 in. (2.5–5 cm.) across, 5 petals resembling a pinwheel; white, pink, rose, or cherry red, often with contrasting eye.
Season: Summer until fall frost; all zones.
When to plant: Sow seeds indoors at 70–75°F (21–24°C) 8–10 weeks before planting-out weather in spring. Keep in continual darkness until they sprout. Outdoors, sow where they are to grow and bloom when soil is warm. Set out transplants when available.
Light: Sunny to partly sunny. Hardly any flower can match the performance of this one in dry summer heat.
Soil: Well drained, moist to on dry side. Caution: Avoid cold—below 60°F (15°C)—and wet conditions.
Fertilizer: 5-10-5.
Uses: Beds, borders, pots.

CELOSIA
(sel-LOW-shah)

Cockscomb

AMARANTHACEAE; amaranth family

Height/habit: Upright; dwarf, 8 in. (20 cm.); medium, 14–16 in. (35–40 cm.); tall, 3 ft. (1 m.).
Leaves: Lanceolate, to 3–4 in. (7.5–10 cm.) long.
Flowers: Crested (cockscomb) to 12 in. (30 cm.) across or plumed to 12 in. (30 cm.) tall; creamy white, yellow, pink, rose, to darkest red.
Season: Summer until fall frost.
When to plant: Sow seeds indoors at 70–75°F (21–24°C) 6–8 weeks before planting-out weather; sow outdoors where they are to grow and bloom when soil is warm. Set out transplants when available. Sowing too early as well as cold temperatures—below 65°F (18°C)—result in premature flowering; all zones.
Light: Sun half day or more.
Soil: Well drained, moist.
Fertilizer: 5-10-5.
Uses: Beds, borders, pots, bouquets, drying.

CENTAUREA
(sen-TAW-ree-ah)

Bachelor's Button; Cornflower; Dusty Miller

COMPOSITAE; daisy family

Height/habit: Dwarf bachelor's button (*C. cyanus*) and dusty miller (*C. cineraria*), 8–10 in. (20–25 cm.) high/wide; standard bachelor's button (cornflower), 1.5–2 ft. (45–61 cm.).

Leaves: Gray-green in bachelor's button, .5 in. (1.2 cm.) wide; 2–3 in. (5–7.5 cm.) long. Silver-gray in dusty miller, deeply cut, lacy; 1–2 in. (2.5–5 cm.) wide, 4–5 in. (10–12.5 cm.) long.

Flowers: 2 in. (5 cm.) across in bachelor's button; blue, mauve, maroon, pink, rose, or white. Dusty miller grown for its silver leaves—the .5-in. (1.2 cm.) yellow flowers are incidental.

Season: Bachelor's button late spring until summer in cold climates; winter until spring zone 8 and warmer. Dusty miller late spring until killing frost.

When to plant: Sow bachelor's button seeds outdoors where they are to grow and bloom in earliest spring or fall zone 8 and warmer. Set transplants when available. Sow dusty miller seeds indoors at 65°F (18°C) 8–12 weeks before planting-out weather. Set out transplants when available.

Light: Sun half day or more.

Soil: Well drained, moist to on dry side.

Fertilizer: 5-10-5.

Uses: Beds, borders, pots, bouquets.

CHRYSANTHEMUM
(kriss-ANTH-ee-mum)

Annual Chrysanthemum

COMPOSITAE; daisy family

Height/habit: Erect bushes, many branches, 1–3 ft. (30–90 cm.) high/wide.

Leaves: Deeply cut or finely divided, 4–6 in. (10–15 cm.) long.

Flowers: Single daisies, 1–3 in. (2.5–7.5 cm.) across; white, yellow, pink, or rose, often bicolored in annual chrysanthemum (*C. carinatum*). Other choice species are *C. multicaule* and *C. paludosum*.

Season: Summer or until frost; all zones.

When to plant: Sow seeds indoors at 65–70°F (18–21°C) 6–8 weeks before planting-out weather; sow outdoors where they are to grow and bloom when soil is warm. Set transplants when available.

Light: Sun half day or more.

Soil: Well drained, moist.

Fertilizer: 5-10-5.

Uses: Beds, borders, pots, bouquets.

CLARKIA
(KLARK-ee-ah)

Farewell-to-spring; Satin Flower; Godetia

ONAGRACEAE; evening prim-rose family

Height/habit: Bushy, upright to sprawling, 1.5–3 ft. (45–90 cm.) high/wide.
Leaves: Lanceolate, to 2 in. (5 cm.) long.
Flowers: Single or double, 2–4 in. (5–10 cm.) across, in loose spikes; white, pink, rose, red, or salmon.
Season: Spring until summer, best in cool weather; all zones.
When to plant: Sow seeds where they are to grow and bloom, fall in mild-winter regions, early spring elsewhere. Set transplants when available.
Light: Sun half day or more.
Soil: Well drained, moist to on the dry side.
Fertilizer: 5-10-5.
Uses: Beds, borders, pots, bouquets.

CLEOME
(klee-OH-me)
Spider Flower
CAPARACEAE; caper family

Height/habit: 2–6 ft. (61 to 180 cm.) high/wide.

Leaves: Compound with 5–7 leaflets, to 5 in. (12.5 cm.) across, on rigid stems with spines.

Flowers: Racemes to 5–6 in. (12.5–15 cm.) across; spidery, ephemeral; white, pink, or cherry rose.

Season: Summer or until killing frost; all zones.

When to plant: Prechill seeds 1 week in refrigerator. Sow seeds indoors at 70–75°F (21–24°C) 8–10 weeks before planting-out weather; sow outdoors where they are to grow and bloom when soil is warm. Set out transplants when available. Often reseeds.

Light: Sun half day or more.

Soil: Well drained, moist to on the dry side.

Fertilizer: 5-10-5.

Uses: Beds, borders, backgrounds, large pots.

CLITORIA
(klih-TOH-ree-ah)
Butterfly Pea
LEGUMINOSAE; pea family

Height/habit: Slender twining vine, 10–20 ft. (3–6 m.).

Leaves: 5–7 leaflets to 4 in. (10 cm.) long.

Flowers: To 2 in. (5 cm.); sea blue or white.

Season: Summer or until killing frost; all zones.

When to plant: Soak seeds 24–48 hours in room-temperature water, then sow indoors at 70–75°F (21–24°C) 12 weeks before warm, frost-free weather arrives. Set out transplants when available.

Light: Sun half day or more.

Soil: Well drained, moist.

Fertilizer: 5-10-5.

Uses: Quick cover for lattice, trellis, arbor, chain-link fence.

COLEUS
(KOH-lee-us)

Painted Nettle

LABIATAE; mint family

Height/habit: 8–20 in.
(20–50 cm.) high/wide.
Leaves: Crenate-serrate, some
with extra cuts and ruffles;
2–4 in. (5–10 cm.) long; many
colors and combinations.
Flowers: Thin blue spikes to
4 in. (10 cm.) long; late summer through fall. Grown
primarily for colorful leaves.
Season: Late spring until fall;
all zones.

When to plant: Sow seeds
indoors at 70°F (21°C) 8–12
weeks before frost-free
weather. Seeds need light to
sprout; do not cover. Set
transplants when available.
Cuttings from favorite plants
carried over the winter in
warmth root easily in spring.
Light: Sunbelt varieties need
a half day or more; others
thrive in part shade.
Soil: Well drained, moist.
Fertilizer: 5-10-5.
Uses: Beds, borders, pots.

CONSOLIDA
(kohn-SOL-id-ah)
Larkspur; Annual Delphinium
RANUNCULACEAE; buttercup family

Height/habit: 2–4 ft. (61–120 cm.).
Leaves: Mostly basal, finely cut.
Flowers: Each about 1 in. (2.5 cm.) across in vertical racemes or panicles; shades of blue, mauve, pink, or white.
Season: Late spring until summer in the North; late winter until spring zone 8 and warmer.
When to plant: Sow seeds in late fall or winter (or earliest spring in the North) where plants are to grow and bloom. Set out transplants when available. Often reseeds.
Light: Sun half day or more.
Soil: Well drained, moist.
Fertilizer: 5-10-5.
Uses: Beds, borders, bouquets.

CONVOLVULUS
(kohn-VOLV-yew-lus)

Dwarf Morning Glory

CONVOLVULACEAE; morning-glory family

Height/habit: Bushy, spreading, 1 ft. (30 cm.) high, 2 ft. (61 cm.) wide.
Leaves: Linear, oblong, to 3 in. (7.5 cm.).
Flowers: Funnelform trumpets, 2–3 in. (5–7.5 cm.) across; blue, white, yellow ('Royal Ensign'), or dark red ('Crimson Monarch').
Season: Summer; flowers open only in sun.
When to plant: First nick seed with file, then plant in warm soil where it is to grow and bloom. Set transplants when available.
Light: Sun half day or more.
Soil: Well drained, moist to on the dry side; tolerates drought.
Fertilizer: 5-10-5.
Uses: Beds, borders, rock gardens, pots.

COREOPSIS
(koh-ree-OP-siss)

Pot of Gold

COMPOSITAE; daisy family

Height/habit: Bushes, 1–1.5 ft. (30–45 cm.).
Leaves: Entire or pinnately lobed, mostly in basal rosettes.
Flowers: Single or double, 2 in. (5 cm.) across; intense yellow. Deadheading increases bloom.
Season: Summer until frost in cold climates; spring until early summer zone 8 and warmer. Cultivars 'Early Sunrise' and 'Sunray' behave as hardy perennials zones 4 and warmer.

When to plant: Sow seeds indoors at 70°F (21°C) 4–6 weeks before frost-free weather; sow outdoors where they are to grow and bloom when soil is warm. Set transplants when available.
Light: Sun half day or more.
Soil: Well drained, moist to on the dry side.
Fertilizer: 5-10-5.
Uses: Beds, borders, pots, bouquets.

CORIANDRUM
(koh-ree-AND-rum)

Coriander; Cilantro (Chinese Parsley)

UMBELLIFERAE; carrot family

Height/habit: Tidy rosettes or clumps, 6–12 in. (15–30 cm.) high/wide.
Leaves: Resemble Italian parsley, to 6 in. (15 cm.) long/wide.
Flowers: Umbels to 1 ft. (30 cm.) above the leaves, lacy; white; followed by seed heads that are the herbalist's coriander.
Season: Leaves in cool weather; flowers beginning of summer; all zones.

When to plant: Sow seeds where they are to grow and bloom in early spring; fall in climates with mild winters. Set transplants when available. Reseeds.
Light: Sun half day or more; tolerates more shade than most herbs.
Soil: Well drained, moist.
Fertilizer: 5-10-5.
Uses: Beds, borders, edging, pots; cilantro leaves for the kitchen.

COSMOS
(KOZ-mose)

Cosmos

COMPOSITAE; daisy family

Height/habit: Bushy, 1-6 ft.
(30–180 cm.)
Leaves: Pinnately cut, 3–5 in.
(7.5–12.5 cm.) long.
Flowers: Single or double,
2–3 in. (5–7.5 cm.) across
in 'Klondyke' types
(*C. sulphureus*, which are
yellow, orange, or mahogany
red); 4-6 in. (10-15 cm.)
across in 'Sensation' types
(*C. bipinnatus*, which are lilac
pink, rose, crimson, or white).
Deadheading increases bloom.
Season: Summer until frost
in cold climates; at almost any
time zone 9 and warmer.
When to plant: Sow seeds
indoors at 70°F (21°C) 4–6
weeks before frost-free
weather; sow outdoors
where they are to grow and
bloom when soil is warm.
Set transplants when available.
Light: Sun half day or more.
Soil: Well drained, moist.
Fertilizer: 5-10-5.
Uses: Beds, borders, pots,
bouquets.

CUCURBITA
(kew-KURB-it-ah)

Gourd

CUCURBITACEAE; gourd family

Height/habit: Tendril-climbing vine, 10–20 ft. (3–6 m.).
Leaves: Coarse, triangular to ovate, lobed, 1–1.5 ft. (30–45 cm.) long/wide.
Flowers: Male and female on same plant, 5-lobed, to 5 in. (12.5 cm.) across; yellow; followed by the fruit in various shapes, sizes, and colors.

Season: Summer until frost.
When to plant: Sow seeds where they are to grow and bloom when soil is thoroughly warm.
Light: Sun half day or more.
Soil: Well drained, moist to on the dry side; tolerates drought.
Fertilizer: 5-10-5.
Uses: Quick cover for fence, trellis, unsightly brush; decorative gourds for household ornament.

DATURA
(dah-TOO-rah)
Angel's Trumpet
SOLANACEAE; nightshade family

Height/habit: Bushy,
spreading, 3–6 ft. (1–1.8 m.).
Leaves: Ovate, entire to den-
tate, 8–10 in. (20–25 cm.) long;
green, grayish, or purplish.
Flowers: Outward-facing
trumpets to 8 in. (20 cm.) long
by 2–3 in. (5–7.5 cm.) across;
white, cream, yellow, purple,
often bicolored and doubled
hose-in-hose style; fragrant.
Season: Summer until frost;
perennial zone 9 and warmer.
When to plant: Sow seeds
indoors at 70–75°F (21–24°C)
8–10 weeks before frost-free
weather. Set transplants
when available.
Light: Sun half day or more.
Soil: Well drained, moist to
on the dry side.
Fertilizer: 5-10-5.
Uses: Beds, borders, pots.

DAHLIA
(DAL-ee-ah)
Annual Dahlia
COMPOSITAE; daisy family

Height/habit: Bushy, 10–18 in.
(25–45 cm.).
Leaves: Pinnate, to 6 in.
(15 cm.) long.
Flowers: Single or double,
2–4 in. (5–10 cm.) across;
most colors except blue.
Season: Summer until frost.
When to plant: Sow seeds
indoors at 70°F (21°C) 12–16
weeks before frost-free
weather; grow seedlings at cool
temperature, 50°F (10°C). Set
transplants when available.
Light: Sun half day or more.
Soil: Well drained, moist.
Fertilizer: 5-10-5.
Uses: Beds, borders, pots,
bouquets.

DIANTHUS
(die-ANTH-us)

Pink; Carnation; Sweet William

CARYOPHYLLACEAE; pink family

Height/habit: Rainbow pink (*D. chinensis*) varieties grown as annuals form 6–8-in. (15–20-cm.) mounds. *D. caryophyllus* as annual garden carnations grow 1–1.5 ft. (30–45 cm.). *D. barbatus* in annual varieties of sweet William grow 6–12 in. (15–30 cm.).

Leaves: Lanceolate, to 2 in. (5 cm.) long; mostly basal, green, or blue-green.

Flowers: Solitary, panicled, or in heads; individuals 1–2 in. (2.5–5 cm.) across; white, pink, rose, red, often bicolored; some clove-scented. Garden carnations are also orange or yellow. Deadheading increases bloom.

Season: Late spring until fall frost in the North; fall until early summer zone 9 and warmer.

When to plant: Sow seeds indoors at 70°F (21°C) 8–10 weeks before planting-out weather; sow outdoors where they are to grow and bloom, as soon as soil is warm. Set transplants when available.

Light: Sun half day or more.

Soil: Well drained, moist to on the dry side.

Fertilizer: 5-10-5. Caution: Do not use ammonia-based fertilizer.

Uses: Beds, borders, edgings, rock gardens, pots, nosegays, bouquets.

(DOLE-ick-os)

Purple Hyacinth Bean

LEGUMINOSAE; pea family

Height/habit: Twining, purple-stemmed vine, 10–30 ft. (3–9 m.).

Leaves: 3 leaflets, 3–6 in. (7.5–15 cm.) long.

Flowers: Resemble small butterflies, to 1 in. (2.5 cm.) across, in loose racemes to 1 ft. (30 cm.) long; lavender purple and fragrant; followed by bright purple pods.

Season: Summer or until frost; all zones.

When to plant: Sow seeds where they are to grow and bloom when soil is warm. Set transplants when available.

Light: Sun half day or more.

Soil: Well drained, moist.

Fertilizer: 5-10-5.

Uses: Quick cover for fence, trellis, arbor, tepee.

DOROTHEANTHUS
(doh-roth-ee-ANTH-us)

Ice Plant; Livingstone Daisy

AIZOACEAE; carpetweed family

Height/habit: Spreading, trailing, 4–6 in. (10–15 cm.) high x 1–1.5 ft. (30–45 cm.) wide.

Leaves: Succulent, thin, tapered, to 3 in. (7.5 cm.) long, green to bluish.

Flowers: Daisylike, to 2 in. (5 cm.) across; pink, white, rose, yellow, often bicolored.

Season: Summer until frost in cold climates; spring until summer zone 9 and warmer.

When to plant: Sow seeds indoors at 65°F (18°C) 8–10 weeks before frost-free weather; provide continual darkness until seeds sprout. Set transplants when available.

Light: Full sun, the more the better.

Soil: Well drained, on the dry side.

Fertilizer: 5-10-5.

Uses: Beds, dry banks/slopes, rock gardens, pots.

DYSSODIA
(diss-OH-dee-ah)
Dahlberg Daisy
COMPOSITAE; daisy family

Height/habit: 8-in. (20-cm.) mounds.

Leaves: Finely dissected, to 2 in. (5 cm.) long.

Flowers: 1 in. (2.5 cm.) across; bright yellow.

Season: Summer until frost in cold climates; winter until spring zone 9 and warmer.

When to plant: Sow seeds indoors at 70°F (21°C) 6–8 weeks before frost-free weather. Seeds need light to sprout; do not cover. Sow fall through early winter in mild climates. Set transplants when available. Often reseeds.

Light: Sun half day or more.

Soil: Well drained, moist to on dry side.

Fertilizer: 5-10-5.

Uses: Beds, border edging, rock gardens, pots, hanging baskets.

EMILIA
(ee-MEE-lee-ah)
Tassel Flower; Flora's Paintbrush
COMPOSITAE; daisy family

Height/habit: Flowering stems thin, wiry, 1.5–2 ft. (45–61 cm.).

Leaves: Mostly in basal rosettes to 6 in. (15 cm.) long, reminiscent of dandelion.

Flowers: Brushlike, rounded, to 1 in. (2.5 cm) across; orange, red, or yellow. Deadheading increases bloom.

Season: Summer or until fall frost; all zones.

When to plant: Sow seeds indoors at 70°F (21°C) 6–8 weeks before frost-free weather; sow outdoors where they are to grow and bloom as soon as soil is warm. Provide continual darkness until seeds sprout. Set transplants when available.

Light: Sun half day or more.

Soil: Well drained, moist to on the dry side.

Fertilizer: 5-10-5.

Uses: Beds, borders, pots, bouquets.

ESCHSCHOLZIA
(esh-SCHOLTZ-ee-ah)

California Poppy

PAPAVERACEAE; poppy family

Height/habit: Mounded, 10–18 in. (25–45 cm.).
Leaves: Dissected finely into segments, blue-green.
Flowers: Single or double, 1–2 in. (2.5–5 cm.) across, borne singly above the foliage; creamy yellow, vivid orange, or salmon pink.
Season: Spring zone 8 and warmer; summer in colder climates.

When to plant: Sow seeds outdoors in late fall or earliest spring where they are to grow and bloom. Transplanting is difficult, but seeds sown directly in 4-in. (10-cm.) pots are often available as transplants; take care not to disturb rootball when setting into garden.
Light: Sun half day or more.
Soil: Sandy, well drained, moist to on the dry side.
Fertilizer: 5-10-5.
Uses: Beds, edging, rock gardens, pots.

EUPHORBIA
(yew-FOR-bee-uh)

Summer Poinsettia; Snow-on-the-mountain

EUPHORBIACEAE; spurge family

Height/habit: Erect bush, 2–4 ft. (61–122 cm.).
Leaves: Resemble those of poinsettia in *E. cyathophora* (*E. heterophylla* of trade, also called summer poinsettia), turning orange-red at the plant tops; white-margined, blue-green in *E. marginata* (snow-on-the-mountain).

Flowers: Inconspicuous.
Season: Summer or until fall frost; all zones.
When to plant: Prechill seeds 1 week in refrigerator, then sow indoors 70°F (21°C) 6–8 weeks before frost-free weather; sow outdoors where they are to grow and bloom as soon as soil is warm. Set transplants when available. Often reseeds.
Light: Sun half day or more.
Soil: Well drained, moist to on the dry side.
Fertilizer: 5-10-5.
Uses: Beds, borders, pots.

FELICIA
(fel-EE-shah)

Blue Daisy

COMPOSITAE; daisy family

Height/habit: Bushy mounds, to 1 ft. (30 cm.) tall/wide.
Leaves: Finely cut, fernlike, 1–2 in. (2.5–5 cm.) long.
Flowers: Single, to 1 in. (2.5 cm.) across; blue with yellow centers.
Season: Winter until spring in mild climates; summer zone 7 and colder.
When to plant: Sow seeds indoors at 68–86°F (20–30°C) 8–10 weeks before planting-out weather; sow outdoors where they are to grow and bloom when soil is warm. Set transplants when available. Reseeds.
Light: Sun half day or more.
Soil: Well drained, moist.
Fertilizer: 5-10-5.
Uses: Beds, borders, edging, rock gardens, pots, hanging baskets.

GAILLARDIA
(gay-LARD-ee-ah)

Blanketflower

COMPOSITAE; daisy family

Height/habit: Bushy mounds, 8–18 in. (20–45 cm.).
Leaves: Mostly basal, linear to lanceolate, often pinnately lobed, 3–4 in. (7.5–10 cm.).
Flowers: Solitary on wiry stems, single or double, 2–3 in. (5–7.5 cm.) across; yellow, orange, red, or mahogany. Deadheading increases bloom.
Season: Summer until frost in cold climates; spring until summer zone 8 and warmer.

When to plant: Sow seeds indoors at 70°F (21°C) 6–8 weeks before frost-free weather; sow outdoors where they are to grow and bloom when soil is warm. Set transplants when available. Often reseeds.
Light: Sun half day or more.
Soil: Well drained, moist to on the dry side.
Fertilizer: 5-10-5.
Uses: Beds, borders, rock gardens, pots, bouquets.

GAZANIA
(gah-ZAY-nee-ah)
Treasure Flower
COMPOSITAE; daisy family

Height/habit: Low mounds, 6–10 in. (15–25 cm.).

Leaves: Form a basal rosette reminiscent of dandelion but waxy; green above, silvery white below, 3–5 in. (7.5–12.5 cm.) long.

Flowers: Solitary on peduncle 6–8 in. (15–20 cm.) long; single daisies to 3 in. (7.5 cm.) across, closing at night and in cloudy weather; white, yellow, orange, pink, or mahogany, often bicolored. Deadheading increases bloom.

Season: Summer until frost in cold climates; spring until fall zone 8 and warmer (where the plants can persist as perennials).

When to plant: Sow seeds indoors at 60°F (15°C) 14–16 weeks before frost-free weather; grow seedlings at 55–60°F (13–15°C). Set transplants when available.

Light: Sun half day or more.

Soil: Well drained, moist to quite dry.

Fertilizer: 5-10-5.

Uses: Beds, edging, rock gardens, ground cover, pots.

GERBERA
(GURB-er-ah)
Transvaal Daisy
COMPOSITAE; daisy family

Height/habit: Mounds 6–12 in. (15–30 cm.) tall/wide.

Leaves: Form basal rosette, reminiscent of dandelion, 4–6 in. (10–15 cm.) long.

Flowers: Single or double, 3–5 in. (7.5–12.5 cm.) across, solitary atop graceful stems, 6–18 in. (15–45 cm.) tall; most colors except blue. Deadheading increases bloom.

Season: Late summer until fall frost in cold climates, late winter until spring zone 9 and warmer (where the plants persist as perennials). Short days initiate flower buds.

When to plant: Sow seeds indoors at 70°F (21°C) 12–16 weeks before frost-free weather. Plant fresh seeds with the pointed end down, other end exposed; they need light to sprout. Grow at 60°F (15°C) nights, 70–75°F (21–24°C) days. Set transplants when available (but do not subject to freezing).

Light: Sun half day or more in cooler climates, shade midday in high temperatures (above 80°F [26°C]).

Soil: Well drained, moist.

Fertilizer: 5-10-5.

Uses: Beds, borders, pots, bouquets.

GILIA
(JILL-ee-ah)

Globe Gilia

POLEMONIACEAE; phlox family

Height/habit: Erect to sprawling, 2–3 ft. (61–90 cm.) high/wide.

Leaves: Finely cut, mostly toward the plant base.

Flowers: Dense in globes, to 1 in. (2.5 cm.) across; long, wiry stems; sky blue.

Season: Summer or until frost; all zones.

When to plant: Sow seeds indoors at 70°F (21°C) 6–8 weeks before planting-out weather; do not cover as light aids germination. Sow outdoors where they are to grow and bloom when soil is warm. Set transplants when available.

Light: Sun half day or more.

Soil: Well drained, moist.

Fertilizer: 5-10-5.

Uses: Beds, borders, pots, bouquets.

GOMPHRENA
(gom-FREE-nah)

Globe Amaranth; Everlasting Bachelor's Button

AMARANTHACEAE; amaranth family

Height/habit: Mounded or bushy, 6–24 in. (15–61 cm.) high/wide.

Leaves: Oblong to elliptic, to 4 in. (10 cm.) long.

Flowers: Dry, globular heads, to 1 in. (2.5 cm.) across; lavender, orange, pink, red, rose, purple, or white.

Season: Summer until fall frost; all zones.

When to plant: Sow seeds indoors at 70°F (21°C) 8–10 weeks before frost-free weather; sow outdoors where they are to grow and bloom after the soil is warm. Set transplants when available.

Light: Sun half day or more.

Soil: Well drained, moist to on the dry side.

Fertilizer: 5-10-5.

Uses: Beds, borders, edging, pots, bouquets, drying.

HELIANTHUS
(hee-lee-ANTH-us)

Annual Sunflower

COMPOSITAE; daisy family

Height/habit: Strongly upright, 2–12 ft. (61–360 cm. [3.6 m.])
Leaves: Ovate, to 1 ft. (30 cm.) long, rough to the touch.
Flowers: Single or double, 3–12 in. (7.5–30 cm.) across; orange, yellow, white, or mahogany.
Season: Summer until frost in cold climates; midspring until early summer zone 8 and warmer.

When to plant: Sow seeds indoors at 70–75°F (21–24°C) 4–6 weeks before frost-free weather, preferably in individual small pots so as not to disturb the roots when planting in the garden; or sow seeds where they are to grow and bloom in the garden as soon as soil is warm. Set transplants when available.
Light: Sun half day or more.
Soil: Well drained, moist.
Fertilizer: 5-10-5.
Uses: Beds, borders, backgrounds, dwarfs in pots, bouquets, edible seeds.

HELICHRYSUM
(hell-ee-CHRISS-um)

Everlasting; Strawflower

COMPOSITAE; daisy family

Height/habit: Tidy clumps
1.5–3 ft. (45–90 cm.).
Leaves: Oblong or lanceolate
to 5 in. (12.5 cm.) long.
Flowers: Composed of dry,
glossy, petal-like bracts, 2–3 in.
(5–7.5 cm.) across; most colors
except blue. Harvest for drying
just before they open fully.
Season: Late spring until early
summer zone 8 and warmer,
summer in cold climates.

When to plant: Sow seeds
indoors at 70°F (21°C)
8–10 weeks before frost-free
weather; sow outdoors where
they are to grow and bloom as
soon as soil is warm. Sow
seeds on surface; they need
light to sprout. Set transplants
when available.
Light: Sun half day or more.
Soil: Well drained, moist.
Fertilizer: 5-10-5.
Uses: Beds, borders, pots,
bouquets; best for drying.

HELIOTROPIUM
(hee-lee-oh-TROPE-ee-um)

Heliotrope; Cherry Pie

BORAGINACEAE; borage family

Height/habit: Bushy to
shrublike, 1–4 ft. (30–122 cm.)
high/wide.
Leaves: Elliptic or oblong to
lanceolate, to 3 in. (7.5 cm.)
long.
Flowers: Coiled cymes,
displaying clusters to 8 in.
(20 cm.) across; deep blue-
violet to purple, lavender,
near-white; legendary
fragrance.
Season: Midsummer to fall
frost in cold climates, late
winter until spring zone 9
and warmer.
When to plant: Sow seeds
indoors at 70°F (21°C) 8–12
weeks before frost-free
weather. Set transplants
when available.
Light: Sun half day or more.
Soil: Well drained, moist.
Fertilizer: 5-10-5.
Uses: Beds, borders, pots,
bouquets.

HELIPTERUM
(hee-LIP-ter-um)

Everlasting; Strawflower; Rhodanthe

COMPOSITAE; daisy family

Height/habit: Erect, 1.5–2 ft. (45–61 cm.) high/wide.
Leaves: Linear to lanceolate, to 3 in. (7.5 cm.) long, bluish green.
Flowers: Papery dry, petal-like bracts; round blooms, 2–3 in. (5–7.5 cm.) across; pink, rose, or white.

Season: Summer; all zones.
When to plant: Sow seeds indoors at 65–75°F (18–24°C) 8–10 weeks before frost-free weather; sow outdoors where they are to grow and bloom as soon as soil is warm. Set transplants when available.
Light: Sun half day or more.
Soil: Well drained, moist to on the dry side.
Fertilizer: 5-10-5.
Uses: Beds, borders, pots, bouquets, drying (harvest buds for drying just as they are about to open).

HUNNEMANNIA
(hun-nee-MAN-nee-ah)
Mexican Tulip Poppy; Golden Cup
PAPAVERACEAE; poppy family

Height/habit: Tidy mounds, 1.5–2 ft. (45–61 cm.) high/wide.
Leaves: Blue-green, finely dissected.
Flowers: Single poppies 2–3 in. (5–7.5 cm.) across; glowing yellow.
Season: Summer.
When to plant: Sow seeds indoors at 70–75°F (21–24°C) 8–12 weeks before frost-free weather; sow outdoors where they are to grow and bloom as soon as soil is warm. Sow seeds on surface; they need light to sprout. Set transplants when available.
Light: Sun half day or more.
Soil: Well drained, moist to on the dry side.
Fertilizer: 5-10-5.
Uses: Beds, borders, pots. Irresistible in the company of blue flowers, such as delphinium, larkspur, forget-me-not, and sage.

IBERIS
(eye-BEER-iss)

Annual Candytuft

CRUCIFERAE; mustard family

Height/habit: Mounded, bushy, 10–18 in. (25–45 cm.) high/wide.
Leaves: Lanceolate, 3–4 in. (7.5–10 cm.) long.
Flowers: Dense umbels 2–3 in. (5–7.5 cm.) across; white, pink, rose, or lavender; sometimes fragrant. Deadheading increases bloom.

Season: Summer in cold climates, late spring until early summer zone 8 and warmer. Best performance with warm days (70°F [21°C]), cool nights (50–60°F [10–15°C]).
When to plant: Sow seeds indoors at 70°F (21°C) for germination (then grow cool, at 50–65°F [10–18°C]), 8–10 weeks before frost-free weather; sow outdoors where they are to grow and bloom as soon as soil is warm. Set transplants when available.
Light: Sun half day or more.
Soil: Well drained, moist.
Fertilizer: 5-10-5.
Uses: Beds, borders, pots, nosegays, bouquets.

IMPATIENS
(im-PAY-shenz)

Busy Lizzie; Patience; Sultana

BALSAMINACEAE; balsam family

Height/habit: Bushy mounds, 8–18 in. (20–45 cm.) high/wide.

Leaves: Lanceolate-ovate to elliptic-oblong, 1–4 in. (2.5–10 cm.) long; green or reddish; New Guinea hybrids often variegated white, cream, pink, or red.

Flowers: Rounded, flattened, 1–3 in. (2.5–7.5 cm.) across, often with prominent, nectar-filled spur; nearly every color except true blue. Annual *I. balsamina* (balsam) flowers appear doubled.

Season: Summer until frost in cold climates; nearly all year zone 9 and warmer.

When to plant: Sow seeds indoors at 70°F (21°C) 8–12 weeks before frost-free weather. Do not cover; seeds need light to sprout. Seeds of annual *I. balsamina* require no special treatment and can be sown where they are to grow and bloom as soon as soil is warm. New Guinea impatiens are often propagated from cuttings. Set transplants when available.

Light: Common impatiens is the top-ranked flower for color in the shade. Annual and New Guinea impatiens require more sun. On average, the cooler the climate, the more direct sun is needed by impatiens. Failure to bloom indicates a need for more sun and blossom-booster fertilizer.

Soil: Well drained, moist.

Fertilizer: 5-10-5.

Uses: Beds, borders, edging, pots.

IPOMOEA
(ipp-oh-MEE-ah)

Morning Glory;
Moonflower;
Cardinal Climber

CONVOLVULACEAE; morning-glory family

Height/habit: Twining climber, 10–30 ft. (3–9 m.). Dwarf bush morning glory forms a mound to 3–4 ft. (1–1.2 m.) high/wide.

Leaves: Variously heart-shaped or shallowly 3-lobed, to 6 in. (15 cm.) across; plain green, sometimes variegated silvery white; finely cut in cardinal climber.

Flowers: 5-lobed funnels, to 4–5 in. (10–12.5 cm.) across; blue, white, red, pink, or rose; often bicolored by edging, stripes, or flecks; sometimes fragrant. Moonflower (*I. alba*) blooms at night; the others are best from dawn until midday heat.

Season: Summer or until fall frost; all zones.

When to plant: Sow seeds where they are to grow, first soaking 24–48 hours in room-temperature water, as soon as soil is warm.

Light: Sun half day or more.

Soil: Well drained, moist to on the dry side.

Fertilizer: 5-10-5.

Uses: Decorative cover for fence, arbor, trellis, tepee.

LATHYRUS
(LATH-er-us)

Sweet Pea

LEGUMINOSAE; pea family

Height/habit: Tendril-climbing vine to 6 ft. (1.8 m.); dwarf bush types 1–2 ft. (30–61 cm.).
Leaves: Blue-green paired leaflets, to 2 in. (5 cm.).
Flowers: To 2 in. (5 cm.) across, 1–4 per peduncle; white, pink, blue, rose, red, maroon, yellow, some bicolored; fragrant. Cutting for bouquets increases bloom.
Season: Late spring until summer in coolest climates; late spring until early summer elsewhere, with the exception of winter to midspring zone 8 and warmer.

When to plant: Soak seeds 24 hours in room-temperature water before planting. Sow outdoors where they are to grow and bloom as soon as soil is warm. Zone 8 and warmer, plant in fall. Set transplants, often available in 4-in.-(10-cm.-) diameter plastic pots, when available; take care not to disturb the roots.
Light: Sun half day or more.
Soil: Well drained, moist.
Fertilizer: 5-10-5.
Uses: Dwarf bush types for beds, borders, pots. Climbers for fence, trellis, arbor, tepees, perhaps paired with such deciduous shrubs as hamelia and beautyberry in zone 8 and warmer.

LAVATERA
(lav-uh-TEER-ah)
Tree Mallow
MALVACEAE; mallow family

Height/habit: Upright, shrublike, 1.5–2 ft. (45–61 cm.) high/wide.
Leaves: Rounded hearts, 2–3 in. (5–7.5 cm.) across; medium green.
Flowers: 5-petaled, glistening, to 3 in. (7.5 cm.) across; rose, pink, or white, often with contrasting veins.
Season: Summer or until frost; all zones.

When to plant: Sow seeds indoors at 70°F (21°C) 8–10 weeks before frost-free weather; sow outdoors where they are to grow and bloom when soil is warm.
Light: Sun half day or more.
Soil: Well drained, moist.
Fertilizer: 5-10-5.
Uses: Beds, borders, pots, quick hedging.

LIMONIUM
(lih-MOH-nee-um)
Statice
PLUMBAGINACEAE; leadwort or plumbago family

Height/habit: Upright clumps, 1–3 ft. (30–90 cm.).
Leaves: Mostly basal, 4–6 in. (10–15 cm.) long, resembling those of dandelion; coarse to the touch.
Flowers: Winged spikelets, dry, papery; blue, lavender, white, yellow, orange, apricot, peach, or rose red, often bicolored. Cut for drying just before they open fully.

Season: Summer; all zones.
When to plant: Sow seeds indoors at 70°F (21°C) 6–10 weeks before frost-free weather; sow outdoors where they are to grow and bloom as soon as soil is warm. Set transplants when available.
Light: Sun half day or more.
Soil: Well drained, moist to on the dry side.
Fertilizer: 5-10-5.
Uses: Beds, borders, pots, bouquets, principally for drying.

LINUM
(LEYE-num)

Annual Flax

LINACEAE; flax family

Height/habit: *L. grandiflorum*
erect, compact, to 2 ft.
(61 cm.).
Leaves: Linear to lanceolate,
1–2 in. (2.5–5 cm.)
long; bluish green.
Flowers: Loose panicles, 1–2 in.
(2.5–5 cm.) across; shades of
red, violet-blue, white with
carmine eye, or rose pink.
Season: Summer in the North;
spring until early summer
zone 8 and warmer.
When to plant: Sow seeds
indoors at 70°F (21°C)
8–10 weeks before frost-free
weather; sow outdoors where
they are to grow and bloom
as soon as soil is warm.
Set transplants when available.
Light: Sun half day or more.
Soil: Well drained, moist to
on the dry side.
Fertilizer: 5-10-5.
Uses: Beds, borders, rock
gardens.

LISIANTHUS
(liss-ee-ANTH-us)

Eustoma; Texas Bluebell

GENTIANIACEAE; gentian family

Height/habit: Erect, small clumps, 1–2.5 ft. (30–75 cm.).
Leaves: Waxy, blue-green, ovate or oblong, to 3 in. (7.5 cm.) long, occurring mostly toward the base.
Flowers: Single or double, resembling Canterbury bells, tulips, rosebuds; 2–3 in. (5–7.5 cm.) across; blue, white, pink, lavender, or rose, often bicolored.

Season: Summer; all zones.
When to plant: Sow seeds indoors at 68–77°F (20–25°C) 10–12 weeks before frost-free weather. Do not cover; seeds need light to sprout. Set transplants when available. (This plant is not easy to grow from seed.)
Light: Sun half day or more.
Soil: Well drained, moist to on the dry side.
Fertilizer: 5-10-5.
Uses: Beds, borders, pots, cutting.

LOBELIA
(loh-BEE-lee-ah)
Edging Lobelia
LOBELIACEAE; lobelia family

Height/habit: *L. erinus*
mounded to trailing, 4–12 in.
(10–30 cm.).
Leaves: Ovate to elliptic,
mostly at the base, narrower at
top; to 1 in. (2.5 cm.) long.
Flowers: 2 upper and 3 lower
lobes, to 1 in. (2.5 cm.) across;
exceptional blues, also lilac,
rose, crimson, or white.
Season: Summer to frost in
cold climates; spring until early
summer zone 8 and warmer.

When to plant: Sow seeds
indoors at 70–75°F (21–24°C)
8–12 weeks before frost-free
weather; sow in fall zone 8 and
warmer. Sow on surface, and
do not cover; seeds need light
to sprout. Grow at cool temperatures: 45–50°F (7–10°C).
Set transplants when available.
Light: Sun half day or more.
Soil: Well drained, moist.
Fertilizer: 5-10-5.
Uses: Beds, borders, edging,
rock gardens, pots, hanging
baskets.

LOBULARIA
(lob-yew-LAY-ree-ah)

Sweet Alyssum

CRUCIFERAE; mustard family

Height/habit: Mounded to trailing, 4–12 in. (10–30 cm.).
Leaves: Linear to lanceolate, gray-green, to 1 in. (2.5 cm.) long.
Flowers: Small, .25–.5 in. (.63–1.25 cm.) on slender pedicels, becoming so numerous as to hide the leaves; white, rose, violet, or purple. Deadheading by periodic light shearing increases bloom.

Season: Summer until frost in the North; late winter to early summer zone 8 and warmer.
When to plant: Sow seeds indoors at 70°F (21°C) 6–8 weeks before frost-free weather; sow outdoors where they are to grow and bloom when soil is warm. Sow fall until winter zone 8 and warmer. Set transplants when available.
Light: Sun half day or more.
Soil: Well drained, moist to on the dry side.
Fertilizer: 5-10-5.
Uses: Beds, borders, edging, pots, hanging baskets.

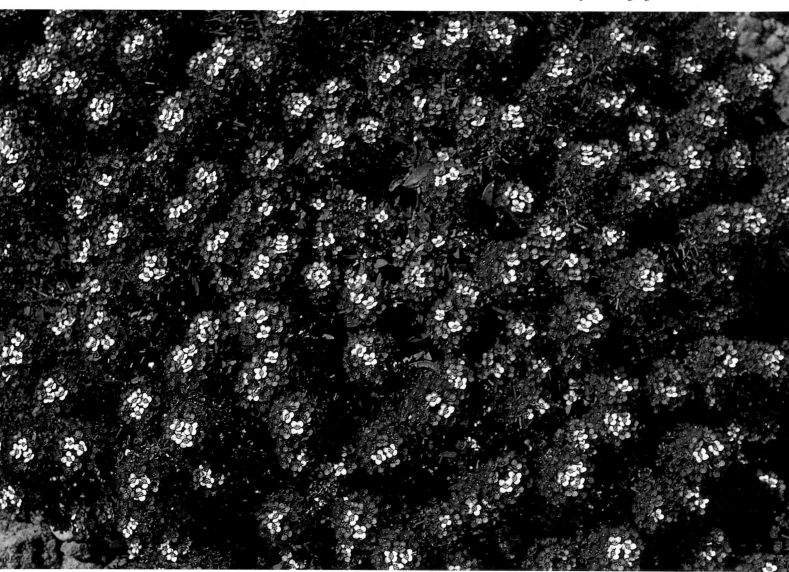

MELAMPODIUM
(mel-am-PODE-ee-um)
'Medallion' Daisy
COMPOSITAE; daisy family

Height/habit: Self-branching mounds, 2–4 ft. (61–122 cm.) high/wide.
Leaves: Heart-shaped, to 2 in. (5 cm.) long.
Flowers: Single, to 1.5 in. (3.7 cm.) across; vivid yellow, bronze-eyed. Self-cleaning (deadheading not required).
Season: Late spring to summer until frost (an outstanding, self-reliant performer over a long season); all zones.

When to plant: Sow seeds indoors at 70°F (21°C) 8–10 weeks before warm weather; darkness needed until seedlings appear, then grow on in high light. Set transplants when available.
Light: Sun half day or more.
Soil: Well drained, moist; when established, tolerates some drought.
Fertilizer: 5-10-5.
Uses: Beds, borders, large pots.

MATTHIOLA
(mat-ee-OH-lah)
Stock
CRUCIFERAE; mustard family

Height/habit: Upright in tidy clumps; dwarfs 8–12 in. (20–30 cm.), standards 2–2.5 ft. (61–75 cm.).
Leaves: Oblong to oblanceo-late, gray-green, to 4 in. (10 cm.) long.
Flowers: Single or double, to 1 in. (2.5 cm.) across, in terminal racemes; pink, purple, red, or white; fragrant. Deadheading increases bloom.
Season: Summer until frost in the North; winter until spring zone 8 and warmer.
When to plant: Sow seeds indoors at 70°F (21°C) 6–8 weeks before frost-free weather; sow outdoors where they are to grow and bloom when soil is warm. Sow late spring until summer or fall zone 8 and warmer. Set trans-plants when available.
Light: Sun half day or more.
Soil: Well drained, moist.
Fertilizer: 5-10-5.
Uses: Beds, borders, pots, bouquets.

MENTZELIA
(ment-ZEE-lee-ah)

Blazing Star; Bartonia

LOASACEAE; loasa family

Height/habit: Upright, vase-shaped, to 2 ft. (61 cm.) high/wide.
Leaves: Waxy, cut or toothed, 2–3 in. (5–7.5 cm.) long.
Flowers: Showy, to 5 in. (12.5 cm.) across; can resemble those of daisy, cactus, or passiflora; creamy white to greenish yellow; some open at night; fragrant.
Season: Summer; all zones.

When to plant: Refrigerate seeds 1 week before sowing. Sow seeds indoors at 70°F (21°C), then grow cool, at 50–65°F (10–18°C), or where they are to grow and bloom when soil is warm. Set transplants when available. Reseeds.
Light: Sun all day.
Soil: Well drained, moist to on the dry side; tolerates drought.
Fertilizer: 5-10-5.
Uses: Beds, borders, wild gardens.

MIMULUS
(MIM-yew-lus)

Monkey Flower

SCROPHULARIACEAE; figwort family

Height/habit: Self-branching clumps, 8–10 in. (20–25 cm.).
Leaves: Heart-shaped to oblong-lanceolate, 3–6 in. (7.5–15 cm.) long.
Flowers: Pouched, 1–2 in. (2.5–5 cm.) across; cream, red, rose, yellow, or wine, often marked with a contrasting color.
Season: Late spring until hot weather; late winter until early spring zone 8 and warmer.

When to plant: Sow seeds indoors at 65–70°F (18–21°C) 8–12 weeks before planting-out weather; grow at cool temperatures, 50–65°F (10–18°C). Zone 8 and warmer, sow fall until winter. Set transplants when available.
Light: Sun early or late in the day, mostly shade; needs more sun in cool temperatures, about 40–60°F (4–15°C).
Soil: Well drained, moist.
Fertilizer: 5-10-5.
Uses: Beds, borders, pots.

MIRABILIS
(mihr-AB-il-iss)

Four-o'clock

NYCTAGINACEAE; four-o'clock family

Height/habit: Upright, branching, to 4 ft. (1.2 m.) high/wide.
Leaves: Heart-shaped to ovate-lanceolate, to 3 in. (7.5 cm.) long.
Flowers: 5-lobed, whorled, growing from a tube, 1–2 in. (2.5–5 cm.) across; white, yellow, red, rose, pink, or salmon, often splashed with a second color. Fragrant blossoms open late afternoon. Self-cleaning (deadheading not required).

Season: Summer or until frost; all zones.
When to plant: Prechill seeds in refrigerator 1 week before planting. Sow indoors at 70–75°F (21–24°C) 6–8 weeks before frost-free weather; sow outdoors where they are to grow and bloom when the soil is warm. Set transplants when available.
Light: Sun half day or more.
Soil: Well drained, moist to on the dry side. Tolerates drought when established.
Fertilizer: 5-10-5.
Uses: Beds, borders, large pots. An outstanding performer in difficult situations.

MONARDA
(mon-ARD-ah)

Lemon Mint

LABIATAE; mint family

Height/habit: Tidy upright clumps of *M. citriodora* grow to 2 ft. (61 cm.).

Leaves: Lemon-scented, narrow lanceolate to oblong, 2 in. (5 cm.) long.

Flowers: Whorled, to 2 in. (5 cm.) across; white to pink and purplish.

Season: Late spring until early summer zone 8 and warmer; summer in cooler regions.

When to plant: Prechill seeds 1 week in refrigerator before planting. Sow indoors at 70°F (21°C) 8–10 weeks before planting-out weather; sow outdoors where they are to grow and bloom when soil is warm. Set transplants when available. Behaves variously as annual or biennial. Reseeds.

Light: Sun half day or more.

Soil: Well drained, moist to on the dry side; tolerates drought.

Fertilizer: 5-10-5.

Uses: Beds, borders, wild gardens, fresh or dried bouquets.

MYOSOTIS
(my-oh-SOH-tiss)

Forget-me-not

BORAGINACEAE; borage family

Height/habit: Thin flowering stems rise above mostly basal foliage, 8–24 in. (20–61 cm.).
Leaves: Oblong to linear or oblong to lanceolate, 2–3 in. (5–7.5 cm.) long/wide.
Flowers: Small, .25 in. (.63 cm.) across, but profuse; blue with white eye, also pink to white. Deadheading increases bloom.
Season: Winter until spring zone 8 and warmer; spring until early summer in colder climates.

When to plant: Sow seeds indoors at 65–70°F (18–21°C) and maintain in continual darkness until they sprout, 6–8 weeks before planting-out weather. In zone 8 and warmer sow seeds in fall. Set transplants when available.
Light: Sun half day or more in cool temperatures (below 60°F [15°C]); provide shade in heat.
Soil: Well drained, moist.
Fertilizer: 5-10-5.
Uses: Beds, borders, pots, bouquets. Recommended for interplanting with spring bulbs (tulip, daffodil).

NEMESIA
(nuh-MEE-zee-ah)

Cape Jewels

SCROPHULARIACEAE; figwort family

Height/habit: Self-branching bushlets to 1–2 ft. (30–61 cm.) tall/wide.

Leaves: Lanceolate to linear, to 4 in. (10 cm.) long.

Flowers: 4-in. (10-cm.) panicles, 1 in. (2.5 cm.) across, pouched; white, yellow, orange, rose pink, scarlet, or crimson, often marked on the outside with darker color.

Season: Early summer until hot weather; late winter until spring zone 8 and warmer.

When to plant: Sow seeds indoors at 65°F (18°C); maintain continual darkness until sprouts appear; grow at cool temperatures, 50–65°F (10–18°C), 8–10 weeks before planting out. Start fall until early winter zone 8 and warmer. Set transplants when available.

Light: Sun half day or more in cool weather; more shade in higher temperatures prolongs season.

Soil: Well drained, moist.

Fertilizer: 5-10-5.

Uses: Beds, borders, pots; ideal for cool greenhouse or frost-free sun-heated pit in fall through winter.

NICOTIANA
(nick-oh-she-YAY-nah)

Flowering Tobacco

SOLANACEAE; nightshade family

Height/habit: Dwarfs in tidy clumps, 1–2 ft. (30–61 cm.). *N. alata, N. rustica, N. sylvestris* are taller, to 3–5 ft. (1–1.5 m.), more graceful.

Leaves: Oval to heart-shaped to elliptic, more growing toward the base, 5–12 in. (12.5–30 cm.) long/wide.

Flowers: 5-lobed, tubular bell-like, to 2 in. (5 cm.) wide x 4 in. (10 cm.) long; white, chartreuse, pink, old rose, wine, or red. Species notably fragrant. Occasional deadheading improves appearance, increases bloom.

Season: Summer or until frost; all zones.

When to plant: Sow seeds indoors at 70°F (21°C) 8–10 weeks before warm weather. Do not cover; seeds need light to sprout. In zone 8 and warmer they can be started in fall; protect in the event of frost. Set transplants when available. Often reseeds.

Light: Sun half day or more in cool season; more shade as temperatures rise.

Soil: Well drained, moist.

Fertilizer: 5-10-5.

Uses: Beds, borders, pots.

NIEREMBERGIA
(neer-em-BERJ-ee-ah)

Cup Flower

SOLANACEAE; nightshade family

Height/habit: Tidy mounds, to 12 in. (30 cm.) high/wide.
Leaves: Linear, to 1 in. (2.5 cm.) long.
Flowers: Shallow cups, 1–2 in. (2.5–5 cm.) across; blue or white.
Season: Summer or until frost in the North; spring until early summer in hottest climates, zones 8–9.

When to plant: Sow seeds indoors at 70–75°F (21–24°C) 8–12 weeks before planting-out weather. Set transplants when available.
Light: Sun half day or more; more shade beneficial in hot weather.
Soil: Well drained, moist.
Fertilizer: 5-10-5.
Uses: Beds, borders, pots, hanging baskets.

NIGELLA
(nigh-JELL-ah)

Love-in-a-mist

RANUNCULACEAE; buttercup family

Height/habit: Bushy, self-branching, upright to sprawling, 1.5–2 ft. (45–61 cm.) high/wide.

Leaves: Finely segmented, similar to dill and fennel, to 3 in. (7.5 cm.) long.

Flowers: Finely laced, spidery, to 2 in. (5 cm.) across; white or pale to dark blue. Deadheading increases bloom but prevents seed capsules prized for drying.

Season: Summer in cold climates; spring until early summer zone 8 and warmer.

When to plant: Prechill seeds in refrigerator 1 week before planting. Sow outdoors where they are to grow and bloom as soon as soil can be worked. Set transplants when available; take care not to disturb roots.

Light: Sun half day or more.

Soil: Well drained, moist to on the dry side.

Fertilizer: 5-10-5.

Uses: Beds, borders, pots, bouquets, drying.

NOLANA
(no-LAY-nah)

Chilean Bellflower

NOLANACEAE; nolana family

Height/habit: Low, spreading mounds, 6–12 in. (15–30 cm.) high/wide.

Leaves: Ovate, obtuse, to 2 in. (5 cm.) long.

Flowers: 5-lobed, to 2 in. (5 cm.) wide; blue with white throat.

Season: Late spring until summer; all zones.

When to plant: Sow seeds indoors at 72°F (22°C) 6–8 weeks before frost-free weather; provide continuous light until seedlings emerge; sow outdoors where they are to grow and bloom when soil is warm. Set transplants when available.

Light: Sun half day or more.

Soil: Well drained, moist to on the dry side.

Fertilizer: 5-10-5.

Uses: Beds, borders, rock gardens, pots, hanging baskets.

OCIMUM
(OH-sim-um)

Basil

LABIATAE; mint family

Height/habit: Bushy, self-branching, 1–6 ft. (30–180 cm.) high/wide.

Leaves: Ovate to ovate-elliptic, .5–5 in. (1.25–12.5 cm.) long; green or red-purple (either color might be streaked or splashed with the other); edible; scents and tastes include sweet basil, lemon, anise, cinnamon, and clove. Thai basil hints of chocolate in both taste and color and makes a beautiful garden plant.

Flowers: Small, borne in spikes above the leaves; white to lavender pink or purplish (usually pinched to keep from forming).

Season: Summer or until frost; all zones. African blue basil often persists through mild winters, zones 9–10.

When to plant: Sow seeds indoors at 70–75°F (21–24°C) 6–8 weeks before warm, frost-free weather; sow outdoors where they are to grow and bloom when soil is warm. Set transplants when available.

Light: Sun half day or more.

Soil: Well drained, moist.

Fertilizer: 10-10-10.

Uses: Beds, borders, edging/hedging, pots; leaves for cookery.

PAPAVER
(pap-PAY-ver)

Iceland, Opium, and Shirley Poppies

PAPAVERACEAE; poppy family

Height/habit: Tendency toward basal foliage, above which the flowers rise on slender stems, 1–4 ft. (30–122 cm.).

Leaves: Cut or coarsely toothed, to 6 in. (15 cm.) long, blue-green in *P. somniferum* (opium poppy).

Flowers: Single to double with shimmery petals, 2–6 in. (5–15 cm.) across; all colors except blue (the fabled blue poppy is *Meconopsis*, a perennial). Iceland poppy (*P. nudicaule*) especially beautiful in yellow, coral, and pink. Shirley poppy (*P. rhoeas*) comes in shades of scarlet, pink, salmon, and white. Opium poppy can be white, delicate pink, red, or purple. Deadheading increases bloom but prevents formation of seed heads for drying.

Season: Late spring until summer in colder climates; spring until early summer zone 8 and warmer.

When to plant: Prechill seeds in refrigerator 1 week before planting. Sow where they are to grow and bloom as soon as soil can be worked in spring; zone 8 and warmer sow in fall. Set transplants when available.
Light: Sun half day or more.
Soil: Well drained, moist.
Fertilizer: 5-10-5.
Uses: Beds, borders, cutting, seedpods for drying (if decorative).

PELARGONIUM
(pel-ar-GO-nee-um)

Bedding Geranium

GERANIACEAE; geranium family

Height/habit: Upright-spreading bushlets, 1–2 ft. (30–61 cm.) high/wide.
Leaves: Rounded, crenate, often encircled by a darker color; primarily green in seed-grown varieties, variously variegated white, cream yellow, orange, mahogany in fancy-leaved cultivars propagated from cuttings.
Flowers: Single or double, in umbels of few or many; most colors except blue and yellow, strong in red, pink, salmon, orange, lavender, and white.

Season: Summer or until frost; all zones. They might go out of bloom in extremely hot, humid weather.
When to plant: Sow seeds indoors at 70°F (21°C) 8–12 weeks before warm weather. Hybrid geraniums come true from seed and start blooming in 3–4 months. Set transplants when available.
Light: Sun half day or more. Midday shade beneficial in torrid regions.
Soil: Well drained, moist to on the dry side.
Fertilizer: 5-10-5.
Uses: Beds, borders, pots, cut for nosegays.

PENSTEMON
(PEN-stem-on)

Beardtongue

SCROPHULARIACEAE; figwort family

Height/habit: Stems upright, in small clumps, 2–3 ft. (61–90 cm.).

Leaves: Mostly basal, 2–3 in. (5–7.5 cm.) long.

Flowers: Loose spikes resembling snapdragon, pouched, to 2 in. (5 cm.) across; most colors except blue and yellow, often with contrasting throat and veins. Deadheading increases bloom and likelihood of perennial behavior.

Season: Summer until frost in cold climates; spring until early summer zone 8 and warmer, where the plants might behave as perennials.

When to plant: Prechill seeds 1 week in refrigerator before planting. Sow seeds indoors at 70°F (21°C) 12–16 weeks before planting-out weather and grow at cool temperatures, 50–65°F (10–18°C). Set transplants when available.

Light: Sun half day or more.

Soil: Well drained, moist to on the dry side.

Fertilizer: 5-10-5.

Uses: Beds, borders, pots, cutting.

PERILLA
(puh-RILL-ah)

Shiso

LABIATAE; mint family

Height/habit: Bushy, self-branching, 3–6 ft. (1–1.8 m.) high/wide.

Leaves: Resemble closely related sweet basil (the herb) but might also be ruffled, to 3 in. (7.5 cm.) long; purple or green.

Flowers: Typical of mint family but not showy. This plant is cultivated primarily for foliage effect.

Season: Summer or until frost; all zones; frequently self-sows in warmer parts of country.

When to plant: Prechill seeds in refrigerator 1 week before planting. Sow indoors at 65–70°F (18–21°C) 6–8 weeks before warm weather; sow outdoors where they are to grow and bloom when soil is warm. Do not cover; seeds need light to sprout.

Light: Sun half day or more.

Soil: Well drained, moist.

Fertilizer: 5-10-5.

Uses: Beds, borders, pots, in Asian cuisine.

PETROSELINUM
(pet-roh-SELL-ih-num)
Parsley
UMBELLIFERAE; carrot family

Height/habit: Tidy clumps or rosettes, to 1 ft. (30 cm.) high/wide first season; bolting to 6 ft. (1.8 m.) spring of second season.

Leaves: Divided, flat, celerylike in Italian, much cut and curled in 'Crispum' varieties, to 1 ft. (30 cm.) long/wide.

Flowers: Flattened umbels, to 6 in. (15 cm.) across, at beginning of second season; greenish yellow.

Season: Low, leafy growth through first summer, living over winter zones 6–7 and warmer; flowers second season, then dies. Reseeds.

When to plant: Soak seeds overnight in room-temperature water, then sow at 70°F (21°C) 6–8 weeks before planting-out weather; sow outdoors where they are to grow and bloom when soil is warm. Set transplants when available.

Light: Sun half day or more; tolerates some shade.

Soil: Well drained, moist.

Fertilizer: 10-10-10 or 5-10-5.

Uses: Beds, borders, edging, pots, leaves for culinary purposes.

PETUNIA
(puh-TOO-nee-ah)
Garden Petunia
SOLANACEAE; nightshade family

Height/habit: Self-branching mounds, bushy to cascading, 1–2 ft. (30–61 cm.).

Leaves: Ovate or ovate-lanceolate, 4–5 in. (10–12.5 cm.) long.

Flowers: Trumpet-shaped, single or double, 2–5 in. (5–12.5 cm.) across; all colors, often edged, striped, or starred with a contrasting color. Some are fragrant.

Season: Summer until fall frost in cold climates; spring until summer zone 8 and warmer.

When to plant: Sow seeds indoors at 70°F (21°C) 8–12 weeks before planting-out weather; sow in fall where winters are mild. Do not cover; seeds need light to sprout. Set transplants when available.

Light: Sun half day or more.

Soil: Well drained, moist.

Fertilizer: 5-10-5.

Uses: Beds, borders, pots, hanging baskets.

Annual Phlox

POLEMONIACEAE; phlox family

Height/habit: *P. drummondii* bushy to trailing, self-branching, 8–24 in. (20–61 cm.).
Leaves: Ovate to lanceolate, to 3 in. (7.5 cm.) long.
Flowers: Cluster to 1 in. (2.5 cm.) across; most colors, often with contrasting eye. Deadheading increases bloom.
Season: Summer in cold climates; spring until early summer zone 8 and warmer.
When to plant: Prechill seeds in refrigerator 1 week before planting. Sow indoors at 65°F (18°C) 8–10 weeks before planting-out weather; sow outdoors where they are to grow and bloom when soil is warm. Set transplants when available. Reseeds.
Light: Sun half day or more.
Soil: Well drained, sandy, moist to on the dry side.
Fertilizer: 5-10-5.
Uses: Beds, borders, ground cover, rock gardens, pots.

PORTULACA
(port-yew-LACK-ah)

Rose Moss; Purslane

PORTULACACEAE; purslane family

Height/habit: Mat-forming, prostrate stems, to 12 in. (30 cm.).

Leaves: Cylindrical to obovate, to 1 in. (2.5 cm.) long.

Flowers: Single or double, shimmery, cupped, 1–2 in. (2.5–5 cm.) across; most colors except blue.

Season: Summer or until frost; all zones.

When to plant: Prechill seeds in refrigerator 1 week before planting. Sow indoors at 70°F (21°C) 6–8 weeks before planting-out weather; sow outdoors where they are to grow and bloom when soil is warm. Seeds sprout best in continual darkness. Set transplants when available. Reseeds.

Light: Sun half day or more.

Soil: Well drained, sandy, moist to quite dry; tolerates drought.

Fertilizer: 5-10-5.

Uses: Beds, borders, ground cover, rock gardens, pots.

RATABIDA
(rah-tah-BID-ah)

Mexican Hat; Prairie Coneflower

COMPOSITAE; daisy family

Height/habit: Bushy, self-branching, 1–2 ft. (30–61 cm.) high/wide.

Leaves: Pinnate, 3–4 in. (7.5–10 cm.) long, growing mostly around the plant base.

Flowers: Distinctive disks surrounded by drooping petals, to 2 in. (5 cm.) across; yellow or brownish red.

Season: Summer; spring zone 8 and warmer.

When to plant: Prechill seeds 1 week in refrigerator before planting. Sow seeds indoors at 70°F (21°C) 8–12 weeks before planting-out weather; sow outdoors where they are to grow and bloom when soil is warm. Set transplants when available. Reseeds. Performs variously as annual/biennial/perennial.

Light: Sun half day or more.

Soil: Well drained, moist to on the dry side; tolerates drought.

Fertilizer: 5-10-5.

Uses: Beds, borders, pots, bouquets.

RESEDA
(REZ-uh-dah)

Mignonette

RESEDACEAE; mignonette family

Height/habit: Sprawling,
1–1.5 ft. (30–45 cm.).
Leaves: Elliptic to spatulate,
2–3 in. (5–7.5 cm.) long.
Flowers: Dense racemes,
to 2 in. (5 cm.) across; greenish
white with yellow or orange
highlights. Grown for
fragrance.
Season: Late spring until
summer or until hot weather;
all zones.
When to plant: Prechill seeds
1 week in refrigerator before
planting. Sow indoors at
70°F (21°C) 6–8 weeks before
planting-out weather; sow
outdoors where they are to
grow and bloom when soil is
warm. Set transplants when
available but do not disturb
roots.
Light: Sun half day or more in
cool temperatures, more shade
with increasing heat.
Soil: Well drained, moist.
Fertilizer: 5-10-5.
Uses: Beds, borders, pots,
bouquets.

RICINUS
(rih-SEE-nuss)
Castor Bean
EUPHORBIACEAE; spurge family

Height/habit: Strongly upright, 5–15 ft. (1.5–4.5 m.).

Leaves: Lobed, to 3 ft. (1 m.) across; green, bronze, or red. Caution: Contact can cause severe skin allergy.

Flowers: Many stamens, no petals, to 1 in. (2.5 cm.) across; orange-scarlet.

Season: Summer until frost; perennial zone 10 and warmer, becoming small tree to 40 ft. (12.1 m.).

When to plant: Sow seeds where they are to grow and bloom when soil is warm and there is no danger of frost. Caution: Seeds poisonous.

Light: Sun half day or more.

Soil: Well drained, moist.

Fertilizer: 5-10-5.

Uses: Border background, garden accent.

RUDBECKIA
(rood-BECK-ee-ah)

Black-eyed Susan; Gloriosa Daisy
COMPOSITAE; daisy family

Height/habit: Tidy clumps, 1–3 ft. (30–90 cm.) high/wide.

Leaves: Mostly basal, ovate to elliptic, 3–6 in. (7.5–15 cm.) long.

Flowers: Single or double, 2–6 in. (5–15 cm.) across; yellow, sometimes vividly bicolored red-brown. Deadheading increases bloom.

Season: Summer until frost; spring until summer zone 8 and warmer. Behaves variously as annual/biennial or short-lived perennial.

When to plant: Sow seeds indoors at 70–75°F (21–24°C) 8–10 weeks before planting-out weather; sow outdoors where they are to grow and bloom as soon as soil is warm. Set transplants when available.

Light: Sun half day or more.

Soil: Well drained, moist to on the dry side; tolerates drought.

Fertilizer: 5-10-5.

Uses: Beds, borders, pots, bouquets.

SALPIGLOSSIS
(sal-pee-GLOSS-iss)

Painted Tongue

SOLANACEAE; nightshade family

Height/habit: Tidy clumps
1–2 ft. (30–61 cm.) tall/wide.
Leaves: Mostly basal; elliptic,
narrow, or oblong, to 4 in.
(10 cm.).
Flowers: Resemble single
petunia, 2–3 in. (5–7.5 cm.)
across; velvety orange, red,
yellow, rose, purple, to near-
blue, netted/veined in contrasting color.

Season: Summer in cool
climates; late spring until
early summer zones 9–10.
When to plant: Sow seeds
indoors at 70–75°F (21–24°C)
12–16 weeks before planting-
out weather. Set transplants
when available.
Light: Sun half day or more.
Soil: Well drained, moist.
Fertilizer: 5-10-5.
Uses: Beds, borders, pots,
bouquets.

SALVIA
(SAL-vee-ah)

Annual Sage

LABIATAE; mint family

Height/habit: Well-branched clumps, 1–3 ft. (30–90 cm.) high/wide.

Leaves: Ovate or lanceolate, 2–4 in. (5–10 cm.) long.

Flowers: Spikes above the leaves, to 2 in. (5 cm.) wide x 6 in. (15 cm.) long; white to blue, all shades of red, purple, pink, rose, or violet. Hybrids of scarlet sage (*S. splendens*), mealycup sage (*S. farinacea*), and Texas sage (*S. coccinea*) are grown primarily as annuals, although they can be perennial in milder regions.

Season: Summer or until frost; all zones.

When to plant: Sow seeds indoors at 70°F (21°C), in continual darkness until they sprout, 8–10 weeks before planting-out weather; sow outdoors where they are to grow and bloom when soil is warm. Set transplants when available.

Light: Sun half day or more.

Soil: Well drained, moist.

Fertilizer: 5-10-5.

Uses: Beds, borders, pots, bouquets.

SANVITALIA
(san-vih-TAY-lee-ah)

Creeping Zinnia
COMPOSITAE; daisy family

Height/habit: Trailing, to 6 in. (15 cm.), spreading 2–3 ft. (61–90 cm.).

Leaves: Ovate to broadly lanceolate, 2–3 in. (5–7.5 cm.) long.

Flowers: Single or semidouble daisies, 1 in. (2.5 cm.) across; yellow.

Season: Summer or until frost; all zones.

When to plant: Sow seeds indoors at 70°F (21°C) 6–8 weeks before planting-out weather; sow outdoors where they are to grow and bloom when soil is warm. Do not cover; seeds need light to sprout. Set transplants when available.

Light: Sun half day or more.

Soil: Well drained, moist to on the dry side.

Fertilizer: 5-10-5.

Uses: Ground cover, rock gardens, hanging baskets.

SCABIOSA
(skab-ee-OH-sah)

Pincushion Flower; Mourning Bride

DIPSACACEAE; teasel family

Height/habit: Erect, 2–3 ft. (61–90 cm.) high/wide.
Leaves: Lanceolate, coarsely toothed, mostly at plant base, to 4 in. (10 cm.) long.
Flowers: Domed clusters with stamens protruding like pins from a pincushion, 2–3 in. (5–7.5 cm.) across; fragrant; reddish purple, pink, salmon, rose, violet-blue. Deadheading increases bloom.

Season: Summer until frost in cooler climates; late spring until early summer zone 8 and warmer.
When to plant: Sow seeds indoors at 70–75°F (21–24°C) 8–10 weeks before planting-out weather; sow outdoors where they are to grow and bloom when soil is warm. Set transplants when available.
Light: Sun half day or more.
Soil: Well drained, moist.
Fertilizer: 5-10-5.
Uses: Beds, borders, bouquets.

SCHIZANTHUS
(sky-ZANTH-us)

Butterfly Flower; Poor-man's Orchid

SOLANACEAE; nightshade family

Height/habit: Tidy, upright clumps, 15–30 in. (38–76 cm.) tall/wide.
Leaves: Pinnately cut and divided, to 6 in. (15 cm.), mostly toward the plant base.
Flowers: Complex, shallow cups to 2 in. (5 cm.) across; pink, lilac, violet, white, or purplish, often bicolored.
Season: Late winter until spring in milder climates; late spring until early summer in warm, temperate climes; summer in cool places.

When to plant: Sow seeds indoors at 70–75°F (21–24°C) 12–16 weeks before frost-free weather; zone 8 and warmer sow in fall. Maintain continual darkness until seeds sprout. Set transplants when available.
Light: Sun half day or more if cool; more shade in warmer weather.
Soil: Well drained, moist.
Fertilizer: 5-10-5.
Uses: Beds, borders, pots.

SENECIO
(suh-NEE-see-oh)

Cineraria; Dusty Miller

COMPOSITAE; daisy family

Height/habit: Cineraria grows 6–18 in. (15–45 cm.) high/wide; dusty miller forms tidy bush, 6–24 in. (15–61 cm.) high/wide.
Leaves: Cineraria (*Senecio* x *hybridus*) has basal foliage that is bright green, broad, oval, to 4 in. (10 cm.) long. The lacy leaves of dusty miller (*S. cineraria*) are gray-silver, to 4–8 in. (10–20 cm.) long/wide.
Flowers: Daisies 1–3 in. (2.5–7.5 cm.) across in dense trusses over plant top in cineraria, sweetly scented; smaller, yellow in dusty miller.
Season: Cineraria in late winter until spring in mild climates; late spring until early summer in the North. Dusty miller summer to frost in North; almost all year zone 8 and warmer.

When to plant: Sow cineraria seeds at beginning of cool but frost-free season; fall until early winter in mild climate; summer elsewhere (overwinter in cool greenhouse). Sow dusty miller seeds 8–12 weeks before planting-out weather. Sow on surface, and do not cover; seeds need light to sprout. Maintain 75°F (24°C) until seedlings appear, then grow in cool temperatures (40–60°F [4–15°C]). Set transplants when available.
Light: Sun half day or more. Shade for blooming cineraria prolongs flowers.
Soil: Well drained, moist.
Fertilizer: 5-10-5.
Uses: Beds, borders, dusty miller especially for edging/hedging, pots.

TAGETES
(tah-JEE-teez)
Marigold
COMPOSITAE; daisy family

Height/habit: Self-branching, bushy, upright, 1–4 ft. (30–122 cm.) high/wide.
Leaves: Fernlike, 2–4 in. (5–10 cm.) long/wide, often strong-scented. Those of Mexican mint marigold (*T. lucida*) grow in zone 9 and warmer.
Flowers: Single or double, 1–4 in. (2.5–10 cm.) across; creamy white to yellow, gold, orange, red, or mahogany. Deadheading increases bloom.

Season: Summer until frost in the North; late winter until summer zone 8 and warmer.
When to plant: Sow seeds indoors at 70°F (21°C) 6–12 weeks before frost-free weather, or sow where they are to grow and bloom when soil is warm. Set transplants when available.
Light: Sun half day or more.
Soil: Well drained, moist.
Fertilizer: 5-10-5.
Uses: Beds, borders, edging/hedging, pots, bouquets. Mexican mint marigold leaves are substitute for French tarragon.

THUNBERGIA
(thun-BERJ-ee-ah)

Black-eyed-Susan Vine

ACANTHACEAE; acanthus family

Height/habit: Twining or trailing vine, 3–15 ft. (1–4.5 m.).
Leaves: Ovate to triangular, to 4 in. (10 cm.) long.
Flowers: Flaring tubes, 1–2 in. (2.5–5 cm.) across; orange, yellow, white, with or without brown-purple eye.
Season: Midsummer until frost in cold climates; winter until spring in mild, frost-free gardens (zone 10).

When to plant: Sow seeds indoors at 70–75°F (21–24°C) 6–8 weeks before planting-out weather; sow outdoors where they are to grow and bloom when soil is warm. Set transplants when available.
Light: Sun half day or more.
Soil: Well drained, moist.
Fertilizer: 5-10-5.
Uses: Cover for fence, lattice, arbor, tepee; also attractive spilling from hanging basket.

TITHONIA
(tith-OH-nee-ah)

Mexican Sunflower

COMPOSITAE; daisy family

Height/habit: Bushy, 3–6 ft. (1–1.8 m.) high/wide.
Leaves: Ovate to triangular, 6–12 in. (15–30 cm.) long/wide.
Flowers: Resemble single dahlia, 2–3 in. (5–7.5 cm.) across; orange-scarlet with yellow center.
Season: Summer or until frost; all zones.

When to plant: Sow seeds indoors at 70°F (21°C) 6–8 weeks before planting-out weather; sow outdoors where they are to grow and bloom when soil is warm. Set transplants when available.
Light: Sun half day or more.
Soil: Well drained, moist to on the dry side; tolerates drought.
Fertilizer: 5-10-5.
Uses: Back of border, hedge, large pots, bouquets.

TORENIA
(tor-EE-nee-ah)

Wishbone Flower

SCROPHULARIACEAE; figwort family

Height/habit: Much-branching bushlets, 1 ft. (30 cm.) high/wide.
Leaves: Ovate, serrate, to 2 in. (5 cm.) long.
Flowers: Pouched, to 1 in. (2.5 cm.) across; blue, pink, purple, lilac, or white, with yellow accent.
Season: Late spring or summer until frost; all zones.
When to plant: Sow seeds indoors at 70°F (21°C) 8–12 weeks before frost-free weather. Set transplants when available.
Light: Sun half day or more if cool; more shade if warm or hot.
Soil: Well drained, moist.
Fertilizer: 5-10-5.
Uses: Beds, borders, edging, pots, hanging baskets.

TRACHYMENE
(TRACKY-meen)

Blue Lace Flower; Didiscus

UMBELLIFERAE; carrot family

Height/habit: Erect to sprawling, 1–2 ft. (30–61 cm.)
Leaves: Lobed, cut, fernlike, 2–4 in. (5–10 cm.).
Flowers: Many in an umbel, to 3 in. (7.5 cm.) across; medium to pale blue. Deadheading increases bloom.

Season: Summer until frost; spring until early summer in torrid zones (9–10).
When to plant: Sow seeds indoors at 65°F (18°C) 8–10 weeks before planting-out weather; sow outdoors where they are to grow and bloom when soil is warm. Set transplants when available.
Light: Sun half day or more.
Soil: Well drained, moist.
Fertilizer: 5-10-5.
Uses: Beds, borders, pots, bouquets.

TROPAEOLUM
(trope-ee-OH-lum)

Nasturtium

TROPAEOLACEAE; nasturtium
family

Height/habit: Bushy, self-
branching, 1–1.5 ft. (30–45
cm.), to climbing/trailing,
4–6 ft. (1.2–1.8 m.).
Leaves: Rounded, peltate,
to 2 in. (5 cm.) across, waxy
green, white-splashed in some
varieties.
Flowers: Irregular, 2–3 in.
(5–7.5 cm.) across, with nectar-
bearing spur; orange, rose
pink, red, or yellow; fragrant;
edible if pesticide-free. Cutting
for bouquets or culinary purposes, as well as deadheading,
increases bloom.

Season: Summer until frost in
the North; spring zone 8 and
warmer (but not hardy below
32°F [0°C]).
When to plant: Sow in
individual pots indoors at 65°F
(18°C) 6–8 weeks before frost-
free weather; sow outdoors
where they are to grow and
bloom when soil is warm.
Set transplants when available.
Light: Sun half day or more.
Soil: Well drained, sandy,
moist.
Fertilizer: 5-10-5.
Uses: Beds, borders, pots,
hanging baskets, bouquets.

VERBENA
(ver-BEE-nah)

Garden Verbena;
Vervain

VERBENACEAE; verbena family

Height/habit: Bushy to creep-
ing-trailing, 1–3 ft. (30–90 cm.).
Leaves: Toothed or cut, 1–3 in.
(2.5–7.5 cm.) long.
Flowers: Flattened spikes,
2–3 in. (5–7.5 cm.) across;
pink, peach, red, rose, purple,
lavender, or blue, often
with white eye. Lilac vervain
(*V. bonariensis*), to 4 ft.
(1.2 m.) tall/wide. Deadheading
increases bloom.
Season: Late spring to fall
frost; winter until early
summer zone 8 and warmer,
where verbena is often
perennial.

When to plant: Sow seeds
indoors at 65°F (18°C) 8–10
weeks before planting-out
weather; sow outdoors where
they are to grow and bloom
when soil is warm. Set transplants when available.
Light: Sun half day or more.
Soil: Well drained, moist to on
the dry side; tolerates drought.
Fertilizer: 5-10-5.
Uses: Beds, edging, pots, hanging baskets, bouquets. Lilac
vervain often used in borders,
where it laces pleasingly
among bolder forms.

VIOLA
(veye-O-lah)

Pansy; Viola

VIOLACEAE; violet family

Height/habit: Bushy, much-branched mounds, 6–12 in. (15–30 cm.) high/wide.
Leaves: Ovate to cordate, 1–2 in. (2.5–5 cm.) long.
Flowers: Rounded, 1–4 in. (2.5–10 cm.) across; most colors, often bicolored; fragrant. Deadheading increases bloom.
Season: Spring until summer in the North; fall until spring zone 8 and warmer.

When to plant: Sow seeds indoors at 70°F (21°C) 12–16 weeks before planting-out weather; provide continual darkness until seeds sprout, then grow cool, 50–65°F (10–18°C), and in full sun. Or sow late summer to early fall where they are to grow and bloom. Set transplants when available.
Light: Sun half day or more.
Soil: Well drained, moist.
Fertilizer: 5-10-5.
Uses: Beds, borders, edging, pots, hanging baskets, bouquets; edible if pesticide-free.

XERANTHEMUM
(zuh-RANTH-ee-mum)

Everlasting; Immortelle

COMPOSITAE; daisy family

Height/habit: Much-branched, 1–2 ft. (30–61 cm.) high/wide.

Leaves: Oblong to lanceolate, to 2 in. (5 cm.) long; silvery.

Flowers: Papery, glossy, single, or semidouble, in heads to 2 in. (5 cm.) across; rose, pink, or white.

Season: Summer or until frost; all zones. Harvest for drying when buds begin opening. Left to dry on the plant, the flowers turn tan or light brown.

When to plant: Sow seeds outdoors where they are to grow and bloom when soil is warm. Set transplants when available.

Light: Sun half day or more.

Soil: Well drained, moist to on the dry side; tolerates drought.

Fertilizer: 5-10-5.

Uses: Beds, borders, rock gardens, pots, bouquets, drying.

ZINNIA
(ZIN-nee-ah)

Common Zinnia; Youth-and-old-age

COMPOSITAE; daisy family

Height/habit: Bushy, upright, self-branching, 1–4 ft. (30–122 cm.) high/wide; bushy trailing, 8–24 in. (20–61 cm.) in *Z. angustifolia* (*Z. linearis* of trade).

Leaves: Oval, clasping stems, 2–3 in. (5–7.5 cm.) long; narrow in *Z. angustifolia*.

Flowers: Single or double, ray petals flat or quilled, 1–8 in. (2.5–20 cm.) across; all colors except blue. Deadheading increases bloom.

Season: Summer until frost in cold climates; spring until summer zone 8 and warmer.

When to plant: Sow seeds indoors at 70–75°F (21–24°C) 6–8 weeks before planting-out weather; sow outdoors where they are to grow and bloom when soil is warm. Set transplants when available.

Light: Sun half day or more.

Soil: Well drained, moist to on the dry side.

Fertilizer: 5-10-5.

Uses: Beds, borders, edging/hedging, pots, bouquets.

Chapter Three

Troubleshooting Guide for Annuals

*T*hough annuals are relatively easy to care for, problems will occasionally beset the gardener. The following are the most common dilemmas with easy solutions provided.

Seedling or transplant wilts, collapses, or falls over at the soil line.

This indicates some kind of rot caused by too much water. When the growing medium stays soggy for too long, the roots die for lack of air.

Occasionally this kind of growth response can be traced to overfertilizing. There is always the possibility that what appears at first to be literally a dead wilt is only an indicator that the plant is badly in need of a thorough soaking. Conversely, plants that appear wilted despite their being in wet soil may recover as they begin to dry out.

Green or variously colored small insects clustered on growing tips.

This indicates the presence of aphids, also called plant lice. They can be rubbed off between the fingers or knocked off with strong sprays of water. The condition is generally not considered a long-term threat.

Few or no flowers despite lots of leafy, apparently healthy growth.

This indicates the need for more sunlight or applications of fertilizer labeled specifically for flowering plants, 15-30-15 for example.

Plant leaves flecked yellowish to grayish, overall lackluster appearance.

An indication of red spider mites, tiny insects that cluster on the leaf undersides and eventually cover every surface with tiny webs. Discourage by spraying the plant undersides with strong streams of water. Spider mites mostly attack plants under stress from lack of water when conditions are hot and dry.

Holes eaten from leaves, flowers gnawed or eaten through, sometimes trails of slime over surfaces.

These are indications of caterpillars, worms, or, in case of slime, slugs and snails. Solutions include hand-picking, lightly salting slugs on sight, setting out beer traps for slugs (low bowls of beer mixed with water), or spraying with safe products labeled for the control of caterpillars or slugs/snails.

Chapter Four

Bringing Annuals Into Your Home

There are myriad tempting flowers that give joy in the garden and offer plenty of material for cutting. In fact, it is the mark of an annual that the more flowers are cut for bouquets, the more the plant will bloom. Cutting fresh flowers regularly and promptly removing the spent blooms—"deadheading"—keeps annuals productive over the longest season possible.

Annual flowers offer three distinct opportunities for enjoying their beauty indoors. If you purchase transplants in six-packs, 4-inch (10-centimeter), or quart- (liter-) size pots, with lots of buds and flowers, enjoy them immediately as table and floor decorations. Their utility pots can be hidden by setting them in baskets, slightly larger clay pots, window boxes, or a glazed ceramic cachepot. Just be sure there is a saucer to catch spills and that each plant is moistened well before it is placed in a temporary indoor garden spot.

A reason for growing of annual flowers is having a bounteous supply of material to cut for bouquets. Some gardeners are casual about this, others pursue flower arranging as an art form. Indeed, no part of the floral kingdom is richer in materials than the annuals.

The final harvest from annuals can consist of dried blossoms, scented herbs, wispy grasses, and elegant seed heads, all laid by during the active growing season for indoor decorations that add to the fall and winter pleasures of burrowing indoors, to celebrate the holidays, and anticipate the arrival of the seed and nursery catalogs that signal a new (and better-than-ever) gardening season.

To create effective arrangements, remember to blend a good balance of flower types.

For example:

- Rounded flowers include china aster, chrysanthemum, calendula, cosmos, dahlia, and bachelor's button
- Spiky flowers include snapdragon, sage, stock, and larkspur
- Flowers with graceful lines include salpiglossis, amaranthus, verbena, and abutilon
- Fragrant annual bouquets consist of candytuft, heliotrope, mignonette, flowering tobacco, petunia, pinks, stock, scabiosa, and sweet pea.

For everlastings arrangements and potpourri, the following air-dried flowers and seed heads are recommended:

- Blackberry lily dried seed heads with strawflowers or lemon mint
- Globe amaranth seed heads with gladiolus leaves or statice
- Sunflowers for displaying whole in still-life container arrangement
- Nigella seed heads with celosia
- Blue everlastings to brighten potpourri
- Calendula to brighten potpourri with shades of orange
- Whole pansy blossoms to add an elegant fillip to potpourri
- Pinks blossoms for adding a clove scent to potpourri

Bibliography

Bailey, Liberty Hyde, and Ethel Zoe Bailey; revised and expanded by the staff of the L.H. Bailey Hortorium. 1976. *Hortus Third*. New York: Macmillan Publishing Co.

Bailey, Ralph; McDonald, Elvin; Good Housekeeping Editors. 1972. *The Good Housekeeping Illustrated Encyclopedia of Gardening*. New York: Book Division, Hearst Magazines.

Graf, Alfred Byrd. 1992. *Hortica*. New Jersey: Roehrs Co.

Greenlee, John. 1992. *The Encyclopedia of Ornamental Grasses*. Pennsylvania: Rodale Press.

Heriteau, Jacqueline, and Charles B. Thomas. 1994. *Water Gardens*. Boston/New York: Houghton Mifflin Co.

Hobhouse, Penelope, and Elvin McDonald, Consulting Editors. 1994. *Gardens of the World: The Art & Practice of Gardening*. New York: Macmillan Publishing Co.

Hobhouse, Penelope. 1994. *On Gardening*. New York: Macmillan Publishing Co.

McDonald, Elvin. 1993. *The New Houseplant: Bringing the Garden Indoors*. New York: Macmillan Publishing Co.

McDonald, Elvin. 1995. *The Color Garden Series: Red, White, Blue, Yellow*. San Francisco: Collins Publishers.

McDonald, Elvin. 1995. *The Traditional Home Book of Roses*. Des Moines: Meredith Books.

Mulligan, William C. 1992. *The Adventurous Gardener's Sourcebook of Rare and Unusual Plants*. New York: Simon & Schuster.

Mulligan, William C. 1995. *The Lattice Gardener*. New York: Macmillan Publishing Co.

River Oaks Garden Club. 1989. Fourth Revised Edition. *A Garden Book for Houston*. Houston: Gulf Publishing Co.

Royal Horticultural Society, The; Clayton, John, revised by John Main. Third Edition. 1992. *Pruning Ornamental Shrubs*. London: Cassell Educational Ltd.

Scanniello, Stephen, and Tania Bayard. 1994. *Climbing Roses*. New York: Prentice Hall.

Schinz, Marina, and Gabrielle van Zuylen. 1991. *The Gardens of Russell Page*. New York: Stewart, Tabori & Chang.

Sedenko, Jerry. 1991. *The Butterfly Garden*. New York: Villard Books.

Sunset Books and Sunset Magazine. 1995. *Sunset Western Garden Book*. Menlo Park: Sunset Publishing Co.

Woods, Christopher. 1992. *Encyclopedia of Perennials*. New York: Facts On File, Inc.

Yang, Linda. 1995. *The City & Town Gardener: A Handbook for Planting Small Spaces and Containers*. New York: Random House.

Jacques Amand
P.O. Box 59001
Potomac, MD 20859
free catalog; all kinds of bulbs

Amaryllis, Inc.
P.O. Box 318
Baton Rouge, LA 70821
free list; hybrid Hippeastrum

Antique Rose Emporium
Rt. 5, Box 143
Brenham, TX 77833
catalog $5; old roses, also perennials, ornamental grasses

Appalachian Gardens
Box 82
Waynesboro, PA 17268
catalog $2; uncommon
woodies

B & D Lilies
330 "P" St.
Port Townsend, WA 98368
catalog $3; garden lilies

The Banana Tree, Inc.
715 Northampton St.
Easton, PA 18042
catalog $3; seeds of exotics

Beaver Creek Nursery
7526 Pelleaux Rd.
Knoxville, TN 37938
catalog $1; uncommon
woodies

Kurt Bluemel
2740 Greene Lane
Baldwin, MD 21013
catalog $2; ornamental grasses,
perennials

Bluestone Perennials
7237 Middle Ridge
Madison, OH 44057
free catalog; perennials

Borboleta Gardens
15980 Canby Ave., Rt. 5
Faribault, MN 55021
catalog $3; bulbs, tubers,
corms, rhizomes

Bovees Nursery
1737 S.W. Coronado
Portland, OR 97219
catalog $2; uncommon
woodies

Brand Peony Farms
P.O. Box 842
St. Cloud, MN 56302
free catalog; peonies

Breck's
6523 N. Galena Rd.
Peoria, IL 61632
free catalog; all kinds
of bulbs

Briarwood Gardens
14 Gully Lane, R.F.D. 1
East Sandwich, MA 02537
list $1; azaleas,
rhododendrons

Brudy's Tropical Exotics
P.O. Box 820874
Houston, TX 77282
catalog $2; seeds,
plants of exotics

W. Atlee Burpee Co.
300 Park Ave.
Warminster, PA 18974
free catalog; seeds, plants,
bulbs, supplies, wide selection

Busse Gardens
5873 Oliver Ave., S.W.
Cokato, MN 55321
catalog $2; perennials

Camellia Forest Nursery
125 Carolina Forest
Chapel Hill, NC 27516
list $1; uncommon
woodies

Canyon Creek Nursery
3527 DIY Creek Rd.
Oroville, CA 95965
catalog $2; silver-leaved plants

Carroll Gardens
Box 310
Westminster, MD 21158
catalog $2; perennials,
woodies, herbs

Coastal Gardens
4611 Socastee Blvd.
Myrtle Beach, SC 29575
catalog $3; perennials

The Cummins Garden
22 Robertsville Rd.
Marlboro, NJ 07746
catalog $2; azaleas,
rhododendrons, woodies

The Daffodil Mart
Rt. 3, Box 794
Gloucester, VA 23061
list $1; Narcissus specialists,
other bulbs

Daylily World
P.O. Box 1612
Sanford, FL 32772
catalog $5; all kinds of
Hemerocallis

deJager Bulb Co.
Box 2010
So. Hamilton, MA 01982
free list; all kinds of bulbs

Tom Dodd's Rare Plants
9131 Holly St.
Semmes, AL 36575
list $1; trees, shrubs,
extremely select

Far North Gardens
16785 Harrison Rd.
Livonia, MI 48154
catalog $2; primulas,
other perennials

Flora Lan Nursery
9625 Northwest
Roy Forest Grove, OR 97116
free catalog; uncommon
woodies

Forest Farm
990 Tetherow Rd.
Williams, OR 97544-9599
catalog $3; uncommon
woodies in small sizes

Fox Hill Farm
P.O. Box 7
Parma, MI 49269
catalog $1; all kinds of herbs

Howard B. French
Box 565
Pittsfield, VT 05762
free catalog; bulbs

Gardens of the Blue Ridge
Box 10
Pineola, NC 28662
catalog $3; wildflowers
and ferns

D. S. George Nurseries
2515 Penfield Rd.
Fairport, NY 14450
free catalog; clematis

Girard Nurseries
Box 428
Geneva, OH 44041
free catalog; uncommon
woodies

Glasshouse Works
Greenhouses
Church St., Box 97
Stewart, OH 45778
catalog $2; exotics for
containers

Gossler Farms Nursery
1200 Weaver Rd.
Springfield, OR 97477
list $2; uncommon
woodies

Greenlee Ornamental Grasses
301 E. Franklin Ave.
Pomona, CA 91766
catalog $5; native and
ornamental grasses

Greer Gardens
1280 Goodpasture Island Rd.
Eugene, OR 97401
catalog $3; uncommon
woodies, especially
Rhododendron

Grigsby Cactus Gardens
2354 Bella Vista Dr.
Vista, CA 92084
catalog $2; cacti and
other succulents

Growers Service Co.
10118 Crouse Rd.
Hartland, MI 48353
list $1; all kinds of bulbs

Heirloom Old Garden Roses
24062 N.E. Riverside Dr.
St. Paul, OR 97137
catalog $5; old garden, English,
and winter-hardy roses

Holbrook Farm and Nursery
Box 368
Fletcher, NC 28732
free catalog; woodies and
other select plants

J. L. Hudson, Seedsman
P.O. Box 1058
Redwood City, CA 94064
catalog $1; nonhybrid flowers,
vegetables

Jackson and Perkins
1 Rose Lane
Medford, OR 97501
free catalog; roses, perennials

Kartuz Greenhouses
1408 Sunset Dr.
Vista, CA 92083
catalog $2; exotics
for containers

Klehm Nursery
Rt. 5, Box 197 Penny Rd.
So. Barrington, IL 60010
catalog $5; peonies,
Hemerocallis, hostas,
perennials

M. & J. Kristick
155 Mockingbird Rd.
Wellsville, PA 17365
free catalog; conifers

Lamb Nurseries
Rt. 1, Box 460B
Long Beach, WA 98631
catalog $1; perennials

Las Pilitas Nursery
Star Rt., Box 23
Santa Margarita, CA 93453
catalog $6; California natives

Lauray of Salisbury
432 Undermountain Rd.
Rt. 41
Salisbury, CT 06068
catalog $2; exotics
for containers

Lilypons Water Gardens
6800 Lilypons Rd.
P.O. Box 10
Buckeystown, MD 21717
catalog $5; aquatics

Limerock Ornamental Grasses
R.D. 1, Box 111
Port Matilda, PA 16870
list $3

Logee's Greenhouses
141 North St.
Danielson, CT 06239
catalog $3; exotics for
containers

Louisiana Nursery
Rt. 7, Box 43
Opelousas, LA 70570
catalogs $3–$6;
uncommon woodies,
perennials

Lowe's Own Root Roses
6 Sheffield Rd.
Nashua, NH 03062
list $5; old roses

McClure & Zimmerman
Box 368
Friesland, WI 53935
free catalog; all kinds of bulbs

Mellinger's
2310 W. South Range Rd.
North Lima, OH 44452
free catalog; all kinds of plants

Merry Gardens
Upper Mechanic St., Box 595
Camden, ME 04843
catalog $2; herbs,
pelargoniums, cultivars
of Hedera helix

Milaeger's Gardens
4838 Douglas Ave.
Racine, WI 53402
catalog $1; perennials

Moore Miniature Roses
2519 E. Noble Ave.
Visalia, CA 93292
catalog $1; all kinds of
miniature roses

Niche Gardens
1111 Dawson Rd.
Chapel Hill, NC 27516
catalog $3; perennials

Nichols Garden Nursery
1190 N. Pacific Highway
Albany, OR 97321
free catalog; uncommon
edibles, flowers, herbs

Nor'East Miniature Roses
Box 307
Rowley, MA 01969
free catalog

North Carolina State
University Arboretum
Box 7609
Raleigh, NC 27695
Propagation guide for woody
plants and lists of plants in
the arboretum, $10; member-
ship permits participation in
worthy plant propagation
and dissemination.

Oakes Daylilies
8204 Monday Rd.
Corryton, TN 37721
free catalog; all kinds
of Hemerocallis

Geo. W. Park Seed Co.
Box 31
Greenwood, SC 29747
free catalog; all kinds of seeds,
plants, and bulbs

Plants of the Southwest
Agua Fria, Rt. 6,
Box 11A
Santa Fe, NM 87501
catalog $3.50

Roses of Yesterday and Today
802 Brown's Valley Rd.
Watsonville, CA 95076
catalog $3 third class,
$5 first; old roses

Roslyn Nursery
211 Burrs Lane
Dix Hills, NY 11746
catalog $3; woodies, perennials

John Scheepers, Inc.
P.O. Box 700
Bantam, CT 06750
free catalog; all kinds of bulbs

Seymour's Selected Seeds
P.O. Box 1346
Sussex, VA 23884-0346
free catalog; English
cottage garden seeds

Shady Oaks Nursery
112 10th Ave. S.E.
Waseca, MN 56093
catalog $2.50; hostas, ferns,
wildflowers, shrubs

Siskiyou Rare Plant Nursery
2825 Cummings Rd.
Medford, OR 97501
catalog $2; alpines

Anthony J. Skittone
1415 Eucalyptus
San Francisco, CA 94132
catalog $2; unusual bulbs,
especially from South Africa

Sonoma Horticultural Nursery
3970 Azalea Ave.
Sebastopol, CA 95472
catalog $2; azaleas,
rhododendrons

Spring Hill Nurseries
110 W. Elm St.
Tipp City, OH 45371
free catalog; perennials,
woodies, roses

Sunnybrook Farms Homestead
9448 Mayfield Rd.
Chesterland, OH 44026
catalog $2; perennials, herbs

Surry Gardens
P.O. Box 145
Surry, ME 04684
free list; perennials, vines,
grasses, wild garden

Terrapin Springs Nursery
Box 7454
Tifton, GA 31793
list $1; uncommon
woodies

Thompson & Morgan
Box 1308
Jackson, NJ 08527
free catalog; all kinds
of seeds

Transplant Nursery
1586 Parkertown Rd.
Lavonia, GA 30553
catalog $1; azaleas,
rhododendrons

Twombly Nursery, Inc.
163 Barn Hill Rd.
Monroe, CT 06468
list $4; uncommon
woodies

Van Engelen, Inc.
Stillbrook Farm
313 Maple St.
Litchfield, CT 06759
free catalog; all kinds
of bulbs

Andre Viette Farm & Nursery
Rt. 1, Box 16
Fishersville, VA 22939
catalog $3; perennials,
ornamental grasses

Washington Evergreen Nursery
Box 388
Leicester, NC 28748
catalog $2; conifers

Wayside Gardens
One Garden Lane
Hodges, SC 29695
free catalog; all kinds
of bulbs, woodies,
perennials, vines

We-Du Nursery
Rt. 5, Box 724
Marion, NC 28752
catalog $2; uncommon
woodies, perennials

White Flower Farm
Box 50
Litchfield, CT 06759
catalog $5; woodies,
perennials, bulbs

Whitman Farms
3995 Gibson Rd., N.W.
Salem, OR 97304
catalog $1; woodies,
edibles

Gilbert H. Wild and Son, Inc.
Sarcoxie, MO 64862
catalog $3; perennials, peonies,
iris, Hemerocallis

Winterthur Plant Shop
Winterthur, DE 19735
free list; uncommon woodies

Woodlanders
1128 Colleton Ave.
Aiken, SC 29801
catalog $2; woodies,
hardy Passiflora

Yucca Do
P.O. Box 655
Waller, TX 77484
catalog $3; woodies, perennials

Thanks especially to these
gardeners and institutions for
providing the subject matter
for my photographs:

Jean Atwater, Spokane, WA

Geo. J. Ball Seed Co.,
West Chicago, IL

Berkshire Botanical Garden,
Stockbridge, MA

British Columbia, University
of, Botanic Garden,
Vancouver, BC

Brooklyn Botanic Garden,
Brooklyn, NY

Burpee Seed Co.,
Warminster, PA

Butchart Gardens, Victoria, BC

Chelsea Flower Show,
London, England

Clause Seed Co.,
Bretigny-sur-Orge, France

Cook's Garden,
Londonderry, VT

Goldsmith Seeds, Gilroy, CA

Karen Park Jennings,
Greenwood, SC

Michael Kartuz, Vista, CA

Logee's Greenhouses,
Danielson, CT

Longwood Gardens,
Kennett Square, PA

Meadowbrook Farms,
J. Liddon Pennock, Jr.,
Meadowbrook, PA

Mercer Arboretum and
Botanic Gardens, Humble, TX

Minnesota, University of,
Landscape Arboretum,
Canhassen, MN

Georgia and Eugene Mosier,
Sewickley Heights, PA

Natchez, MS, private garden

National Wildflower Research
Center, Austin, TX

George W. Park Seed Co., Inc.,
Greenwood, SC

Peckerwood Gardens,
Waller, TX

Pier 39, San Francisco, CA

Roger's Nursery and Garden
Center, Corona del Mar, CA

Sissinghurst Castle Garden,
Kent, England

Sluis & Groot,
Enkhausen, Holland

South Coast Botanic Garden,
Peninsula, CA

Strybing Arboretum,
San Francisco, CA

Wave Hill Gardens, Bronx, NY

Index

U.S.D.A. Plant Hardiness Zone Map

Average Annual Minimum Temperature

Temperature (°C)	Zone	Temperature (°F)
-45.6 and below	1	below -50
-45.6 and -45.5	2a	-45 to -50
-40.0 to -42.7	2b	-40 to -45
-37.3 to -40.0	3a	-35 to -40
-34.5 to -37.2	3b	-30 to -35
-31.7 to -34.4	4a	-25 to -30
-28.9 to -31.6	4b	-20 to -25
-26.2 to -28.8	5a	-15 to -20
-23.4 to -26.1	5b	-10 to -15
-20.6 to -23.3	6a	-5 to -10
-17.8 to -20.5	6b	0 to -5
-15.0 to -17.7	7a	5 to 0
-12.3 to -15.0	7b	10 to 5
-9.5 to -12.2	8a	15 to 10
-6.7 to -9.4	8b	20 to 15
-3.9 to -6.6	9a	25 to 20
-1.2 to -3.8	9b	30 to 25
1.6 to -1.1	10a	35 to 30
4.4 to 1.7	10b	40 to 45
4.5 and above	11	40 and above

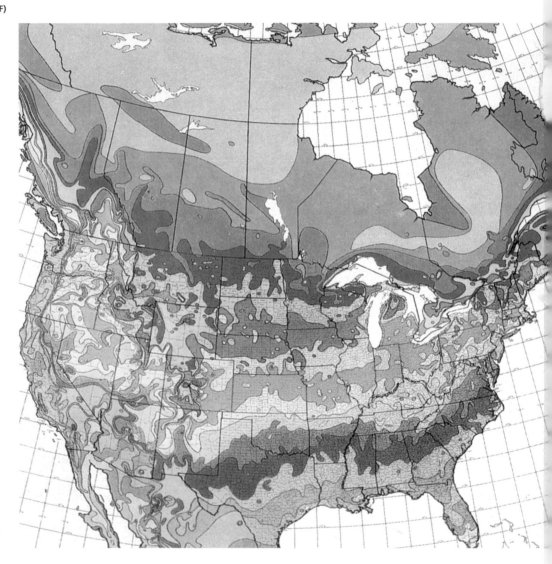

This map, issued by the United States Department of Agriculture, lists average annual minimum temperatures for each zone. It relates directly to the cold-hardiness of plants, but does not address the other extreme, high temperatures. Special considerations with regard to these matters are noted as appropriate throughout the pages of this book.
A new map, in preparation by the U.S.D.A. in cooperation with the American Horticultural Society, will treat equally matters of hot and cold and their effect on plants.